CRIMINAL RECORDS

Criminal Records

State, citizen and the politics of protection

BILL HEBENTON
Lecturer in Criminology
University of Manchester

TERRY THOMAS
Lecturer in Social Work
Leeds Metropolitan University

Avebury

Aldershot · Brookfield USA · Hong Kong · Singapore · Sydney

Published by
Avebury
Ashgate Publishing Limited
Gower House
Croft Road
Hants
GU11 3HR
England

Ashgate Publishing Company
Old Post Road
Brookfield
Vermont 05036
USA

Electronic Typesetting by
Mandy Barrow
Techprint Publishing
Faculty of Health and Social Care
Leeds Metropolitan University
Calverley Street
Leeds LS1 3HE

A CIP catalogue record for this book is available from the British Library

ISBN 1 85628 318 6

Printed and Bound in Great Britain by
Athenaeum Press Ltd., Newcastle upon Tyne.

Contents

Preface and Acknowledgements

Neither of us are quite sure about the genesis of our mutual interest in the subject matter of this book. Suffice it to say that the book has been long in the gestation, and as one would expect we owe a debt to many individuals who have given of their time and knowledge. We specifically mention some of these people below, but for those forgotten in the roll-call – we apologize in advance and simply hope that they may recognize somewhere in this book their particular contribution.

We wish to thank the following: Tim Treuherz, Steve Wright, Sarah Buckmaster and others of the erstwhile Police Checks Monitoring Group, Terry Waller, Madeleine Colvin (Liberty), Sarah Mann (Home Office), DCI McAllister and DI Lamont (New Scotland Yard), the Office of the Data Protection Registrar, James Rule, Gillian Douglas, Carol Kaplan (US Bureau of Justice Statistics), Sheila Barton (Project SEARCH), Jon Somerton, Inge Zurrendonck (Netherlands Ministry of Justice), Stuart Watson and Mandy Barrow for assistance with production of the book, and Alice Mahon MP for asking all those questions. In addition, we acknowledge the helpful discussion of some of our research as presented in papers to the annual conferences of the European Group for the Study of Deviance and Social Control in Ormskirk and Potsdam, and the informal discussions with colleagues in the Department of Social Policy, University of Manchester and Faculty of Health and Social Care, Leeds Metropolitan University. We also owe a debt of gratitude to staff of numerous libraries: the John Rylands University Library of Manchester, the Leeds Metropolitan University Library, Manchester's Central Reference Library, the Public Record Office at Kew and last but not least the redoutable

British Library Document Supply Centre at Boston Spa. It is also fitting at this point to thank the editor of Avebury, Jo Gooderham for taking the risk.

We must also express our thanks to our respective families for their forbearance and considerable assistance: to Sandy, Jessica, Christine, Angus, Helen and Jane a big thank you. Finally, an acknowledgement that this book could probably have been written by either one of us – but the enjoyment of researching it together was more than either of us could resist.

We dedicate this book to all our loved ones – past, present and future.

Bill Hebenton,Manchester
Terry Thomas, Leeds
September 1992

"I also reminded myself that it would probably not be worth the trouble of making books if they failed to teach the author something he hadn't known before, if they didn't lead to unforeseen places, and if they didn't disperse one toward a strange and new relation with himself".

Michel Foucault, Preface to *The History of Sexuality* Volume II.

1 Introduction

The record, the person and society

Each of us, in our own way, tries on occasion to divest ourselves of the baggage of the past. In so doing we intend this personal 'year zero' to be the springboard for better times; a space to re-align what we think we are with what we want to be – it is a project to re-make our own identity. However, other than in the unfortunate case of clinical fugue state victims, this project never quite materialises. Instead, our identity emerges from a complex convergence of responses and perceptions of others, together with information from 'recorded' sources. At the end of the 20th century, we live in a world where recorded sources are increasingly reconstituting the individual. The ability of the state and private organisations to gather information is extending ever deeper into the social fabric. The rationale for this activity is not reducible or determined. It is, instead, better analysed as a form of political rationality. In this book we argue, along with social theorists such as Foucault and Poulantzas, that this modern form of power is normative, develops anticipatory strategies to reduce risk, and presents an essentially diffuse panoptic vision. Some have coined aspects of this 'new surveillance', (Burnham 1983, Marx 1985: 26-34) with computers being accorded a transformational role in the nature of surveillance. Here, record-keeping is routinized, broadened and deepened, and for practical

1

purposes, records become eternal. Bits of scattered information that in the past did not threaten the individual's privacy and anonymity are now-joined.

Contemplating modern social life one can only but share Rule's contention that:

> "Any member of a modern highly 'developed' society is apt to feel that he inhabits two worlds at once. One is the ordinary social world of wants, people, relationships, and so on as they impinge directly on experience. The other is a 'paper world' of formal documentation which serves to verify, sanction and generally substantiate the former, experiential reality."
>
> (Rule 1973: 13)

A vision of this dual world can be seen in Stanton Wheeler's *On record*. Sub-titled, 'Files and dossiers in American life', this book of readings, published at the end of the 60's made a significant contribution to the privacy debate of that era. In it, Wheeler observes:

> "From one perspective, written records are merely one type of information that may serve as a basis for action. There are obviously other types. We all make direct observations about people as we go about our daily routines, and those observations often provide a basis for our actions. In addition, we learn about people indirectly, either through face-to-face conversation or by means of devices like the telephone. but increasingly in American life, the information upon which we act is drawn neither from direct observation nor informal communication, but from consulting the record about the person in question."
>
> (Wheeler 1969: 4)

As Wheeler documents, the process of record-keeping has a number of distinctive characteristics: it installs significance; it creates a permanence; it is autonomous and exists as an 'other' from the person to whom it relates; it allows for combination and 'mixing'. Compiling of records raises problems and issues about the flow of information regarding people that are quite different from those raised by other means of communication:

> "Because records thus affect both the course of an individual's life and the course of society, they present a problem of social significance."
>
> (Wheeler ibid: 5)

It is this 'problem' of social significance which this book seeks to explore by looking at one kind of record-keeping activity, namely criminal records. As we show in later chapters, there is abundant evidence that criminal records have an impact on an increasingly large proportion of the population and more importantly that the making, keeping and disclosure of records is in itself a form of conduct deserving of greater study. In so doing, the book presents a window on wider matters and we connect our concerns with the growth of bureaucratic surveillance (Dandeker 1990) and increased regulation and 'governmentability' of our lives (eg. Rose 1990). While in Jaques Ellul's 'technological society' (Ellul 1964) the individual's life is absorbed, we see the individual as being reconstituted by the discourse of record-keeping, and the power of modern political rationality under pinned by continual monitoring of daily life, adjusting and readjusting ad infinitum the norm of individuality.

Systems of detailed personal records do not appear ' just whenever' we are dealing with large numbers of people. Instead, as cogently argued by James Rule (Rule 1973) they develop under conditions of complex organisations and extended mutual dependency between a social organisation and its public. The conditions most propitious to this activity are:

"1. When an agency must regularly deal with a clientele too large and anonymous to be kept track of on a basis of face-to-face acquaintance.

2. When these dealings entail the enforcement of rules advantageous to the agency and potentially burdensome to the clientele.

3. When these enforcement activities involve decision making about how to act towards the clientele...

4. When the decisions must be made discriminatingly, according to precise details of each person's past history or present situation.

5. When the agency must associate every client with what it considers the full details of his past history, especially so as to forestall people's evading the consequences of their past behaviour". (Rule 1973: 29)

The criminal record

Before going on to an overview of the book and how we have tried to approach this subject it is perhaps worth taking some time to consider what exactly we mean by criminal records. For our purposes the term criminal records is taken as an umbrella term that covers a variety of categories of personal information, that ranges from convictions at court hearings through to speculative information stored by way of police criminal intelligence.

The first category of straight records of court judgements is the list of convictions that we are most familiar with as a given criminal record. The list enables us to identify a given person and to know the date and place of the hearing, the allegations made by way of charge or summons and the resulting sentence that follows a finding of guilt. In the UK such records, as we shall see, are divided into recordable and reportable offences.

A second category of information is that which arises in connection with the police procedures prior to a decision to bring the circumstances before a court. In the USA for example, there has been a higher degree of access to arrest records as a form of public record, whether or not there is a subsequent charge or summons. In the UK this has not been such a visible area to public scrutiny and 'due process' and 'visible' justice more likely to be postponed to the public forum of the court.

A further form of criminal record arising from police procedures is that which decides that a court hearing is not necessary even though an offence has been committed and the person concerned has admitted as much. The use of cautions by the UK police in these circumstances may vary in their degree of formality, but there is a record kept of cautions when administered at their most formal; such cautions may be retrieved or disclosed at a later date in a court or other appropriate forum. The cautioning of offenders as a means of avoiding a court hearing is usually an acknowledgement of the offence being minor or a judgement being made that no 'public interest' will be served by a formal court hearing. Cautions are often part of a policy of 'diversion' to keep young people, mentally disordered people or even elderly people out of the perceived stigmatising process of the public court hearing. For present purposes we should note that some cautions administered by the police may well reappear later as part of a formal criminal record.

Criminal intelligence forms the final category of criminal record under consideration. By its very nature criminal intelligence is difficult to quantify as it varies enormously from police authority to police authority and constitutes any information the police think may be useful in terms of crime prevention or crime detection. The subjectivity involved makes it vary from information on the modus operandi of known criminals, through to involvement in perceived subversive political activities, sexual orientation, subscriptions to certain magazines or simply court cases that resulted in acquitalls or where the prosecuting agencies decided to withdraw charges. In the UK the police are known to keep special indexes of those thought to be involved with child pornography or with violent activities at football matches.

It is clearly difficult to be precise about the extent and nature of criminal intelligence and not least because of the veil of confidentiality thrown around it by those who hold it. For it to be non-confidential, it is argued, would be to undermine those very crime prevention and detection activities for which it is kept. What is clear, and what we illustrate in later chapters, is that the police in the UK increasingly see criminal intelligence and the criminal record as indistinguishable. As John Newing, a lead officer on UK police computerisation has said:

> "There are compelling arguments – financial and operational– in support of having all criminal information on a single data base. It should include not only a person's criminal history, and descriptive features, but also method and general intelligence items." (Newing 1987)

After further developments of the national criminal intelligence computer system, Newing was able to add that:

> "The criminal record, identifiers and intelligence are part of a connected whole. They can be tackled separately but separate development does not address the overall requirement. Future development should be within a framework that aims to provide a fully integrated National Criminal Information and Identification System (NCIIS)." (Newing 1990: 13)

As with most historical analyses it is not easy to define precisely when or where the criminal record was first instituted, but in Chapter 2 we trace the development of national criminal records in Europe and the USA and show how several factors determined content and forms of accountability to government. While in the UK it can be said that Henry and John Fielding undertook the first attempts at establishing the importance of criminal records, (Babington 1969) it is not until 1869 that we have the establishment of a national criminal register. In France in 1850 the criminal record was established and hailed as an ingenious and humanitarian method (it replaced branding) for providing the courts with information on an accused person's background. And in the USA the historical picture is more heterogeneous, with uneven developments at both state and federal level. But by the end of the 19th century, we have in the USA the nucleus of what has now developed into the largest criminal databank in the world – the FBI Identification Division.

Chapter 3 examines the nature of these criminal record systems, and illustrates how they have grown by immense proportions in the last twenty years. In 1971 the FBI's computerised clearinghouse of criminal justice information, the National Crime Information Centre (NCIC) contained about 2.5 million records; now it stores more than 17 million and handles 1 million transactions a day. In addition, the other sources of FBI criminal records, the Automated Identification Division System, launched in 1973, now contains 10 million criminal history records and is increasing by 15,000 records per week

(Gordon 1986). In the UK criminal records are held on 5 million files stored at the National Identification Bureau in London, (House of Commons 1990 (a)) costing some £16 million annually to administer and with a staff of 700.

Chapter 3 in addition to describing the systems, also examines the concerns about the accuracy of information held, its completeness, the concept of 'data quality' and confidentiality. There is an expectation that records will be complete and accurate and that there is a proper match of record with person concerned. We, however, reveal the likely need for new identification measures such as extension to finger-printing and the potential of DNA print databanks as a means of responding to concerns. The book relates these issues to the principles on data protection set out in the Council of Europe's Convention of 1981.

In relation to confidentiality, concerns have existed for a number of years, and we examine the background to these concerns, highlight the civil liberties issues and argue that an adequate understanding depends on deconstructing questions of accountability and the nature of public response. Flaherty in his 1986 review, for example, has shown that no primary legislation on protecting data files in Europe or the USA has been as a result of what one can call 'popular demand' (Flaherty 1986(a)). Legislation in the USA has veered in the 1970s and 1980s from open access to criminal records to restricted access and all framed by a complex public response.

In the UK, the guiding principle has been "that police information should not be disclosed unless there are important considerations of public interest to justify departure from the general rule of confidentiality" (Home Office 1986a). While as we explain fully in Chapters 4 and 5, there are official disclosures of information from records both within and outside the criminal justice system, it is worth noting the problem of 'informal' disclosure.

Several commentators describe the misuse of records, and unauthorised disclosures (see eg. Bunyan 1976: Campbell and Connor 1986). Private tracing agencies, for example, employed ex-policemen familiar with requests to criminal record offices, and who – given the demands on offices – experienced little difficulty because of the impossibility of verifying every call. And drawing on research from the 1970s, it is easy to see examples of the 'Old Pals Act' in operation:

"The vulnerability of those offices (CROs) is especially great to former members of the police, who are inevitably well versed in the techniques of making such requests. Industrial firms employ retired policemen in large numbers as security officers, precisely because of their familiarity with police routines and these and other matters. In many cases too, the personal ties between these private security officers and former colleagues make it possible for them to obtain services which would be denied to others."

(Rule 1973: 82)

We illustrate, with evidence from case-studies and empirical survey research, that despite the increased emphasis on data protection by the police, this unauthorised disclosure continues to the present. What is at stake here is not a simple matter of civil liberties, but the wider issue of what should and should not be private. One imagines that certain behaviour, like committing a crime, involves the rest of society and hence creates a licence for surveillance, for example, in the form of criminal record-keeping. Other behaviour, such as sexual behaviour among consenting adults, may be considered to concern only those who engage in it, and hence not to justify others' attentions. This doctrine has its problems from a philosophical point of view, but it does seem to support a commonsense distinction of considerable importance. The trouble is that current information exchange praxis works to erode the very distinction between public and private in this regard. It does this by turning up unexpected connections between highly personal, and hitherto private data and social behaviour in which others claim a legitimate interest.

Chapters 4 and 5 detail the development of the disclosure of records to other parts of the criminal justice system and to agencies outwith it. We take the view that such arrangements require far greater attention paid to them, (see e.g. Laudon 1986) not only because of the implications for the large proportion of the population with convictions[2], but also because of the considerable expansion of such disclosure in the last twenty years (Thomas and Hebenton 1990).

In chapter 4 we describe not only the nature and extent of disclosure but also the problems with current arrangements and how this is impacting, in the UK context, on court decisions about bail and sentencing; and therefore affecting the justice available from the criminal justice system.

To provide a focus on the uses to which criminal records are put in the criminal justice system we examine two substantive matters: sentencing and jury vetting. On sentencing, few people would be likely to argue with the proposition that a defendant's criminal record is an important determinant of his sentence. Standard legal texts and empirical studies of sentence decision-making in the UK and USA indicate that sentencing outcome is crucially affected by prior record. The modern American sentencing guidelines movement selects the defendant's criminal record (or 'criminal history score') as one of the key determinants in sentencing (Von Hirsch 1981). As we show, however, what is remarkable is that despite virtually unanimous acceptance of the importance of the association between the two, there is a lack of analysis of precisely what information about a defendant's prior record is relevant to sentence selection, and in what ways the influence is manifested. We examine a number of factors which are potentially relevant, such as similarity and frequency of offence. And as a background to some of the issues to be raised in Chapter 6, we conclude by reviewing the literature on the criminal record and prediction together with the role of 'just desserts' philosophy. We tease out two strands in relation to prior record – 'predictive' sentencing and 'just desserts'. It is argued that these approaches are in tension with each other, often entailing contrary inferences from facts about a defendant's previous record (Wasik and Pease 1987). So long as English sentencing retains both approaches in this context, its attitude to the relevance of prior convictions is bound to be incoherent.

Jury vetting, the practice of carrying out checks on the backgrounds of jurors (Enright and Morton 1990), shows that throughout the late 1970s and 1980s, several police forces in the UK were routinely vetting all criminal cases, in clear breach of the then existing Attorney-General's guidelines. Other forces were more circumspect, although it is clear that in many cases low ranking officers were carrying out checks at their own initiative. In the leading case of *R. v Mason,* (3 A11 ER 777 1980) the Court of Appeal legitimised vetting to the extent that the prosecution may unearth criminal convictions with a view to weeding out disqualified jurors together with those jurors whose records may not actually disqualify but suggest that they may be biased. We take this case and critically examine how the Association of Chief Police Officer's recommendations that followed it attempted to re-frame the debate and sanction existing Chief Constable discretion on vetting.

Chapter 5 sets out the intricacies, concerns and public policy issues that arise from the police disclosure of criminal records to bodies outwith the criminal justice system. In the UK there never has been a statutory duty on the police to maintain records of convictions. Indeed, it is not until the Rehabilitation of Offenders Act 1974 that we find some formal recognition of police records, when there is reference to the concept of disclosure of 'official record'[3] However, everyone has long accepted that records would be kept and produced by the police. From this perspective, in the UK at least, criminal records are essentially police records, with the ultimate decision on content and disclosure resting with the relevant Chief Constable. As we illustrate, this discretion is all but unfettered[4].

We show that disclosure arrangements to outside agencies has, in the UK, grown from administrative arrangements – usually departmental circular. This aspect of government-by-circular is critically examined, and we contrast this with the US experience where case and constitutional law did not overly concern itself with the conditions of access attaching to criminal records. Indeed, it is not until the mid 1970s that the US Privacy Act steered a path alongside access to records with the official view that, "criminal justice records are so different in use from other kinds of records, that their disclosure should be governed by separate legislation" (Belair 1988).

Chapter 5 also raises the very real issue of the likely impact of disclosure arrangements within a criminal justice system which itself can operate in a discriminatory manner. Drawing on theoretical insights from critical criminology and empirical studies of sentencing of black people in the UK and USA, together with criminalisation of certain sexual behaviour, we review the case that records act as a hidden stratifier in the economy.

We suggest that such disclosure is all the more in need of careful scrutiny, when we consider the extent to which dependence on criminal background checks has already penetrated social life. Mostly such disclosures relate to certain categories of employment, but they also apply to applicants for various licenses and in a range of other circumstances. On the basis of our own research, we show that, in the UK since 1973, arrangements for the police to disclose criminal background information and pass on details of convictions to employers has doubled.

Bearing in mind the sensitive nature of criminal records, it would seem appropriate that any uses of them should be determined as matters of general public interest and privacy. Within this, we conclude Chapter 5 by trying to answer a series of questions:

- What sort of information should a national criminal records system contain?
- What type of criminal record should be held?
- How can national criminal records be kept accurate and up to date?
- To whom should national criminal records be disclosed?
- What limitations should be placed on the use of criminal records once disclosed from the national system?
- What safeguards should be established for individuals?

As an extended case study of the issues raised in previous chapters we go on in Chapter 6 to examine the disclosure of criminal records in relation to those seeking employment with children. In the 1950s, as we illustrate from an analysis of Home Office files from that era, there were various concerns that 'unsuitable' individuals would seek employment with children. Our analysis shows how common themes present 30 years ago are still with us in terms of public policy and presentation. The 1986 arrangements introduced "procedures for checking with local police forces for the possible criminal background of those who apply or move to work with children" (Home Office 1986 (b)). We analyse the implications of these procedures based on Home Office guidelines to local authorities, health authorities and other bodies. It is argued that these particular disclosure arrangements must be critically situated within the context of an understanding of the relationships between regulatory systems, the private family, children's sexuality and rights and the concept of rehabilitation and dangerousness.

It would be our contention that what we are witnessing is the coming together of a largely shared set of assumptions and meanings, making up a moral universe in which a new 'politics of protection' has arisen. The state had traditionally been accorded a 'protective' role to those members of society, including children, who are more vulnerable than others. The piecemeal developments of criminal record disclosure, bureaucratic demands and technological developments, from the point of view of our analysis, makes the meaning of 'protection' by no means self explanatory. 'Protection' is arguably now, more than ever, assuming the role of metaphor in societies increasingly attempting to grapple with citizenship and the more general question of the individual and the State. 'Protection' is now used in a number of seemingly disparate discourses on social policy and at the same time links these discourses with their instantiation within the State. Protection or pro-active work is now seen as a crucial element of social policy strategy, as in the areas, for example, of crime prevention and combatting child abuse. In so doing, 'at risk' forms part of the discourse for an ever widening set of targets – at risk children, at risk individuals, at risk families, at risk neighbourhoods and at risk communities.

Developments in police co-operation in the European Community are likely to impact with developments in information exchange and in the final chapter we describe current thinking both from the point of view of the police and government on future trends. The issues surrounding police held criminal records in the UK is now of prime importance because of the perceived need to develop common information systems on a Europe-wide basis. The Home Affairs Committee (House of Commons 1990 (b)) concluded as part of its recommendations that the UK Government begin work on European wide standards of disclosure arrangements on the use of criminal records for these 'vetting' purposes. We try to demonstrate, however, that this will be no easy task, primarily because legislation in practice relating to criminal records and the rehabilitation of convicted persons varies so widely in the Member States of the Council of Europe and of the European Community. Authorities responsible for central criminal records in Europe vary from Ministries of Justice, Public Prosecutors, High Courts and the Police themselves. There is currently a debate in the UK on the need for an independent panel to develop policy on disclosure arrangements. Added to this is the variation in the contents of information held as 'criminal records' which in some countries includes such information as decisions to deprive people of their parental rights or decisions regarding guardianship. The picture is further confused by the wide divergences that can be found on allowed periods for automatic rehabilitation.

We conclude with the analysis of likely trends in the USA and the UK in relation to criminal information systems and the extension of disclosure arrangements. As part of this review we scrutinise the concept of an independent criminal records authority (Home Office 1991) as a means of ensuring accurate and up to date records, good practice on disclosure and effective accountability.

Notes

1   The mid and late 1960s saw an avalanche of academic and public concern. See, for example, "Computerisation of Government files: What impact on the individual?" *UCCL Law Review* 1968 15 (No.5): US House of Representatives, Committee on Government operations, Special Sub-Committee on Invasion of Privacy. *The Computer and invasion of privacy: hearings before the Sub-Committee* 89th Congress Second Session July 26-28 1966 Washington D.C. Government Printing Office 1966.

2   See the Home Office cohort studies (eg. Statistical Bulletin 7/85) that indicate that some one third of males have had at least one conviction by the age of 31.

3   Namely "A record kept by ... any police force ... being a record containing information about persons' convictions of offences" (Rehabilitation of Offenders Act 1974 s.9(11)).

4   There is in some countries legal constraints on discretion. For example, the 1984 Data Protection Act prohibits disclosure of information held on computer other than in accordance with registration of the system.

2 The historical background

Everything begins with a plan...

In this chapter we examine the origins of criminal records in England and Wales and the USA. Any attempt at such a task necessitates synthesizing a large volume of historical scholarship into a few pages – however, our aim here is to identify and abstract the key factors which can be said to have underpinned the form and content of criminal record systems.

In August 1753 London magistrate Henry Fielding was sent for by the Duke of Newcastle and asked to attend at his house in Lincoln Inn Fields on business of importance (see Pringle 1955: 104-106). Fielding, who by then was gravely ill, begged to be excused; but the next day the messenger returned with another summons, and he made the effort and went to Newcastle House. He was asked to propose a plan that could be laid before the Privy Council "for putting an immediate end to those murders and robberies which were every day committed in the streets" (Pringle ibid: 104). According to Pringle:

> "Fielding took four days of intense, concentrated labour to draw up his plan, which he says occupied many sheets of paper. Unhappily they have not survived, and the plan was too secret to be printed; if the contents had leaked out it might have brought the Government down. Even after it had

been put into effect, and its benefits made obvious, the public was told very little about it. It was not until some years after Henry's death that the substance of the plan was published by his half brother John. ...His plan was not just an emergency measure designed to get rid of the existing gangs of street robbers: it was a blueprint for a police force".

(Pringle ibid: 105)

A key element of the plan was the proposal that a register should be kept at Bow Street of all crimes reported and all persons suspected, charged, or convicted. This aspect of Henry Fielding's plan was developed, after his death, by his half-brother John Fielding and the Bow Street records remained the earliest and most complete attempt to establish a criminal record system in England (the Bow Street records were destroyed in the Gordon riots of 1780).

Incapacitating the habitual criminal

While in the latter half of the 18th century the Fieldings' work failed to generate greater interest, by the middle of the 19th century the context had changed. The perception of a mass of offenders, mobile yet anonymous, fostered an escalating fear of a dangerous criminal class – vast, self-contained, self-perpetuating and largely irreclaimable. What were the elements in this changed context? Simply put, the new elements were the refusal of Britain's eastern colonies to accept any more convicts, combined with the rapid growth of the cities and an expansion of the police. All combined to make the crime phenomenon appear more acute.

Before 1800 the Home Office possessed few records of criminal trials beyond some rare and scanty returns ordered by Parliament. During the first quarter of the 19th century, when the spirit of reform was very active, additional returns were required from time to time to meet the needs of various select committees. In 1805 clerks of courts and keepers of prisons were required to submit annual returns of persons committed for trial at Great Sessions, Assizes and Quarter Sessions. They gave details of the number of persons committed to various prisons, the number sentenced to death and the number executed. After 1823 the court returns as a source of criminal statistics were supplemented by after-trial calendars. As the name indicates, this calendar is produced after the court is over and lists those who appeared before the court and the decision of the court. In 1823 advantage was taken of a general prison act to make it compulsory for keepers of prisons to send after-trial calendars to the Home Office. The calendar was to contain the name, crime(s) and sentence(s) of every person tried at the session. The calendars were originally in manuscript in a great variety of forms and sizes but in 1834 keepers of prisons were required to send printed calendars.

One of the factors which made the after-trial calendar sufficient as a record of convictions was the tendency for an individual to live the whole of his life in one parish even after serfdom was abolished. The Elizabethan Poor Law system made each parish responsible for its paupers and in consequence the overseers of the poor took good care to ensure that no-one settled in the parish if he might become a burden to it. It was not until 1795 that an act was passed making persons irremovable from the parish until they were actually in need of poor relief. Some movement of persons did, of course, occur but they were usually either those who were unlikely to become a burden because of wealth or because they possessed a certificate from their home parish accepting poor law responsibility for them if required, or they were those who migrated to the large towns where the movement of individuals could not be effectively controlled. After the Poor Law Amendment Acts of 1834, 1844 and 1868 the Poor Law restriction to mobility ceased to apply. To some extent this was merely a recognition of changes resulting from the Industrial Revolution and the Napoleonic Wars. With the building of the railways mobility increased even further. Given such population mobility, it could no longer be assumed that the majority of offenders were known in the locality in which they lived and that any previous convictions against a person could be found recorded in the calendars of his locality.

The abandonment of transportation and its replacement by penal servitude created further problems. Although the offender was usually sentenced for a period of years under the transportation system, he often remained in the colony after that period because the opportunities to make a fresh start were better than in his own country; the period of ticket of leave in that colony made the transition from convict to free man easier and the conditional pardon granted before the expiry of his sentence required him not to return to Britain. When penal servitude was first established in 1853 it was the intention that even though the period in separate confinement and the period of public works might be performed in this country, the period on 'licence to be at large' was to be spent in a colony. In the event, it became increasingly necessary for the period on licence to be spent at home in Britain. A licensee could have his licence revoked so it was necessary to know whether a person was a licensee. Once a person with a previous sentence received an additional or heavier sentence if ever convicted again, as for example under the 1827 Administration of Justice Act and the 1864 Penal Servitude Act, it became necessary to know whether he had any previous convictions. Whereas such information was available in the after-trial calendars this was only relevant if the place, date and name under which convicted were known. Given the tendency for ex-convicts to remove themselves from the area in which they were known and give false names it was not possible any longer to rely on local knowledge and records.

As Radzinowicz and Hood (1990) point out, the problem of incapacitating the habitual criminal through the granting and revoking of licences proved awkward in practice because of the lack of a central record system. When asked by the Home Office in 1862 to report on ticket-of-leave men, Sir Richard Mayne Commissioner of the Metropolis was compelled to acknowledge that, owing to various subterfuges such as changes of residence, "the police could not find or produce a single man of them." (Radzinowicz and Hood 1990: 249). A similar set-back occurred in Birmingham where the police were only able to find 14 ticket-of-leave men out of an estimated 80 to 100 (Radzinowicz and Hood ibid: 250).

Much debate in the mid 1860s revolved around the merits of the Irish convict system, which had, as its final stage, registration and close supervision by a prison official in Dublin and by the police in the country districts. In Ireland since 1859 a system had operated whereby the details (including photographs) of all persons remanded in custody who were suspected of being habitual criminals were forwarded to the Convict Prisons Directors and compared with details of earlier convicts. This system was reputed to bring to notice all those who had previously been convicts. In December 1868, against a backdrop of leading articles in *The Times* (see 2 December: 6, 22 December: 7, 30 December: 6) a deputation to the Home Office headed by Sir Walter Crofton the originator of the Irish system pressed for measures of increased police supervision of habitual criminals. On 26 February 1869 the Earl of Kimberley in introducing the Habitual Criminals Bill (see *Parliamentary Debates*, H.L., 3rd series, vol.194, cols 332-350), pointed out that the strategy of the Bill was to attack problems of supervision on all fronts – to tighten the conditions of the ticket-of-leave; to register all persons convicted of crime. Within six months the hastily drafted 1869 Habitual Criminals Act was passed, following closely on the Irish system.

Section 5 of the Act provided for two registers to be established; one in London under the management of the Commissioner of Police of the Metropolis; and one in Dublin under the Dublin Police Commissioners. These registers were to be kept "in such a form, with such evidence of identity, and containing such particulars, and subject to such regulations as may from time to time be prescribed" by the Secretary of State. The expenses of the registers were to be paid out of monies provided by Parliament.

Section 6 of the 1869 Act required prison governors and chief constables to send details "in such a manner and at such a time, and containing such evidences of identity and other information with respect to persons convicted of crime" as the Secretary of State may from time to time direct and ruled that the expenses of so doing were expenses for the maintenance of the police, and thus to be defrayed locally.

Section 7 laid down that for the purposes of registration of criminals, 'crime' meant any felony or offence and was not limited to the felonies or offences specified in the first schedule of the Act which related to powers of supervision. As will be seen later, this clause was to create difficulties because of the sheer number of cases being included.

The Habitual Criminals Register

Following the passing in August 1869 of the Habitual Criminals Act, the Commissioner of the Metropolis wrote to the Home Office on 21 September 1869 saying that "In accordance with the instructions of the Secretary of State for the Home Department that I should undertake the duty of keeping a Register of all persons convicted of crime in England...I have to submit...the Forms in which I think such Registry ought to be kept.". He gave his view that the then ordinary system of register books would be enormously cumbrous and that there would be a great saving of time and expense, as well as effectiveness, if the records were kept in separate papers for each person with, in addition, an alphabetical register showing the names, aliases and descriptions of all persons convicted. On procedure it was suggested by the Commissioner that each chief constable of police in England and Wales should send by post every Monday a form in respect of each person convicted in that police district during the previous week. If police required information about any suspicious person in custody, application was to be made to the Habitual Criminals Register Office at 4, Whitehall Place, London. Prison governors were to be required to send a form in respect of any criminal convicted of any offence specified in the Schedule who was to be released from prison either on expiry of his sentence or on licence (see figure 1 for an example of part of a circular letter sent by the Home Office in November 1869 – Public Record Office HO 45 9320). After Home Office approval for the proposed procedures, the first returns were received in the Register Office in December 1869, and the first application made for information from the Office on 1st May 1870.

As historians have pointed out the 1869 Act had been pushed through Parliament so hastily that within a year many deficiencies and ambiguities in the legislation appeared. These deficiencies related almost entirely to the police supervisory functions of those on licence and were thought so serious that a new statute was drafted to repeal and virtually re-enact it. This new 1871 Prevention of Crimes Act came into force in November 1871 and as far as register arrangements were concerned it made important changes. The most

Figure 1

CIRCULAR.

WHITEHALL,

8th November, 1869.

Sir,

I AM directed by Mr. Secretary Bruce to transmit to you a copy of the Habitual Criminals Act, passed in the last Session of Parliament, and to call attention to those of its provisions which affect the Police and Governors of Prisons.

The Act has been framed with a view to the protection of the Public from the depredations of detected Offenders by restraining them from relapsing into their old habits of Crime. For this purpose greatly increased powers have been entrusted to the Police, and Mr. Bruce is sure that you will feel the importance of impressing upon all members of the Police Force of your jurisdiction, the necessity which exists for the utmost vigilance and discretion in the exercise of those powers.

While the first object of the Act is undoubtedly the speedy apprehension and punishment of relapsed Criminals, Mr. Bruce wishes it to be ever borne in mind that its powers can and should be so exercised as not only not to interfere with, but as far as possible, to assist the efforts of those who evince a desire to return to an honest life by earning an honest livelihood.

The term " Chief Officer of Police " applies to any Chief Constable, Head Constable, or other Chief Officer of any County, Borough and place maintaining a separate Police Force of its own, and in Counties it applies as well to the Superintendents having charge of Divisions.

The following points appear to Mr. Bruce to demand special attention, viz. :—

That the apprehension without warrant of a Licence Holder (Section 3) who is suspected to be getting a livelihood by dishonest means ;—

The apprehension of a person subject to the supervision of the Police (Section 8) upon a similar suspicion ;—and

The entry without Search Warrant (Section 11) into any premises in search of stolen goods, can only be made by a Constable or other Police Officer under the written authority of the Chief Officer of Police as defined above ; and a fresh authority must be given in each case which may arise.

For the better supervision of Criminals, a register of all persons convicted of Crime in Great Britain will be kept in London ; and Mr. Bruce has, under important changes were that provision was made for a register in Scotland; that no provision was made for chief constables to report convictions although prison governors were still required to report discharges; and that the power to require photographs to accompany the reports was made explicit. On the running costs of the Registers, Section 6 of the Act provided that "The expense of keeping the register...shall, to such extent as may be sanctioned by the Treasury, be paid out of moneys provided by Parliament.". This 1871 Prevention of Crimes Act (as amended in 1876) was to be the basis of centralised records in Britain until its repeal in 1967. An example of particulars of several individuals issued by the Criminals' Register Office and reproduced in the *Police Gazette* of week ending 12th October 1872 is shown in figure 2 (Public Record Office – HO 44 58).

During 1874 a Home Office official, G. Lushington, reviewed the working of the Habitual Criminals Register and obtained reports from the Registrars for Scotland and Ireland. In a letter of 22 June 1874 the Metropolitan Police Commissioner pointed out to the Home Office that 117,568 cases had been registered up to the end of 1873 and that if it was allowed to grow at the current rate of 30,000 a year the Register would grow to half a million names by 1885. Yet there were only 3,957 enquiries of which over 75 per cent were made by the Metropolitan police and in all only 890 identifications had been made. The majority of the registrations referred to summary convictions and that out of a sample of 350 "50 were Juvenile Offenders from 10 to 16 years of age, convicted of Stealing Oranges, Lemonade, Sweetmeats and Ginger Beer." The Commissioner suggested that if the registration was to be continued it should be limited, as in Scotland, to conviction by a jury of the crimes listed in the 1869 Act and estimated this would reduce the number of registrations by three-quarters. He declared in his letter of 22 June "My own opinion is that the Registry Office as now constituted has proved a failure for all useful purposes and that it has only succeeded in getting together a mass of papers of very little value".

Lushington in his report of 1st January 1875 indicated that the Habitual Criminals Register had been a fair success in Ireland with 35.5 per cent of the searches being successful but it had been a comparative failure in England (22.5 per cent) and almost a nullity in Scotland (4.5 per cent). In consequence he concluded that either the system should be abolished or it should be completely reconstructed. He felt that it was easy to form an exaggerated conception of the importance of the Habitual Criminals Registry. It was at most merely paper assistance and as such it served only to a minor degree to supplement police activity. In his view detection must usually depend on the police energetically following up the special circumstances of each case. The Register had greater

Figure 2

POLICE GAZETTE.

CRIMINALS' REGISTER OFFICE.

Particulars of Persons to be Liberated from Prisons in England and Wales during the ensuing WEEK ending 12th October, 1873, and sentenced to Police Supervision under the provisions of Section 8 of the "Prevention of Crimes Act, 1871."

Official Register Number.	Name and Alias.	Description.						Prison from which Liberated, and Date of Liberation.	Offence for which Convicted.	Sentence.	Period for which subject to Police Supervision.	Intended Residence after Liberation.	Marks and Remarks.
		Age	Height	Hair.	Eyes.	Face.	Trade or Occupation.						
B 5309	Prisner Buckland, alias Mary Buckland	30	5 8½	black	hazel	sallow	labourer	Taunton 9 10 73	Larceny, simple	6 months	3 years	Bristol	Left middle finger deformed, mole under right jaw
B 8054	George Blake	41	6 6	dark	hazel	swarth	labourer	Reading 8 10 73	Larceny, simple	6 months	3 years	Cheves, Berks	Woman's head right arm
D 311	Arthur Davidman	30	5 7½	dk. brn	blue	fresh	sawyer	Winchester 8 10 73	Larceny, simple	6 months	3 years	Aldershot	Scars left shoulder and neck. Two previous convictions for felony
D 1511	John Smith, alias Alfred Dickes, Walter Walker	32	5 4	dk. brn	hazel	fresh	hawker	Lewes 10 10 73	Larceny, person	7 months	3 years	Not known	Both feet mutilated from spavin. Two previous convictions for felony
D 5403	Mary Deaves, alias Davies	19	4 10½	sandy	blue	pale	charwoman	Liverpool 11 10 73	Larceny, simple	8 months	7 years	24, Middle street, Liverpool	Birth mark under right eye, scar left chin
D 3303	Emma Dudley, alias Giles	36	5 1½	lt. brn	grey	fresh	servant	Portsmouth 8 10 73	Larceny, dwelling	9 months	7 years	43, Maitland street, Landport, Hants	Birth mark under right eye, scar left chin
F 154	William Farrall, alias Farthing	47	5 8	brown	grey	fresh	labourer	Northallerton 8 10 73	Felony	6 months	3 years	Whitby, York	Cut on nose and left of forehead, right thumb nail split
G 3897	William Greenhow	32	5 10	brown	grey	fresh	clerk	Preston 9 10 73	Larceny, simple	6 months	7 years	Blackborn, Lancashire	Scar right eyebrow, left elbow, mole left arm
H 720	George Hill	27	6	dk. brn	grey	fresh	labourer	Lindsey 11 10 73	Larceny, simple	6 months	1 year	Winterton, Lincoln	Lost top right forefinger, bugle and anchor right arm
K 3308	Mary Ann Hoare	44	5 2	grey	hazel	fresh	—	Portsmouth 11 10 73	Larceny, simple	6 months	7 years	49, Rugles - street, Southsea, Hants	Cut and burn left arm. Nine previous convictions for felony. Previously sentenced to Police Supervision, see Gazette, 31st October, 1870
H 4754	Isaac Hughes	33	5 3	brown	blue	fresh	labourer	Liverpool 7 10 73	Larceny, simple	9 months	7 years	Not known	Cut right eyebrow, nose broken
J 1700	Ellen Jones	18	5 6	brown	grey	fresh	servant	Maidstone 9 10 73	Fraud	6 months	3 years	Servant's Home, Albion Hill, Brighton	Scar right of face
L 3637	Henry Lawrence	29	5 8½	black	dk. brn	medium	labourer	Petworth 10 10 73	Larceny, simple	6 months	5 years	St. Pancras, Chichester, Sussex	Large dark lump wrist eye. Two previous convictions for felony
L 1150	Thomas Lovell	21	5 6	brown	blue	fresh	boat keeper	Liverpool 7 10 73	Larceny, simple	9 months	7 years	12, Tunnel road, Edge Hill, Liverpool	Cut right of forehead, bridge of nose, and left thumb

19

value, according to Lushington, as a means of tracing an arrested person's previous convictions than in identifying habitual criminals.

Although Lushington felt that the Register was not indispensable, he recognized that as far as it contributed to the detection of crime and the award of an appropriate punishment, the system must indirectly help to prevent crime. He accepted that it was important that persons who were convicted twice of crime were recorded in the Register so that the police could be told who they were and where they lived. In essence, Lushington concluded that the prime purpose of the Habitual Criminals Registry was to act as a central information office.

Lushington recommended that the English Register ought to be retained but be put on a better footing. Among the improvements he suggested were that the Register be transferred to the Home Office; that the number of persons to be registered and photographed for inclusion in the Register be reduced by excluding certain summary convictions; that the prison governors be given legal power to photograph prisoners and examine their bodies; that the Irish system of separate male and female registers be adopted; that each register should contain separate lists of persons subject to licence, persons subject to supervision, and habitual prisoners; and that a photograph with its corresponding register entry should be made prima facie evidence of identity. The Lushington report of January 1875 was accepted by the Home Office and the Habitual Criminals Register was transferred from the Commissioner of Police for the Metropolis to the Home Office within twelve months.

As has already been noted the Habitual Criminals Act of 1869 required all persons discharged from prison following a conviction for crime to be reported to the Habitual Criminals Register and the Prevention of Crimes Act 1871 did not change this. In order to reduce the number of cases reported for registration an amendment to the law was necessary and this was done in the Prevention of Crimes Amendment Act 1876 which provided, inter alia, that the Secretary of State could from time to time by order prescribe the class or classes of prisoner to which enactments of the Amendment Act should apply.

On March 15 1877 the Home Office sent a letter to the Justices enclosing a copy of Revised Regulations under the Prevention of Crimes Act 1871 and the Prevention of Crimes Amendment Act 1876. The letter said that up to the present time all persons convicted of 'crime' as defined by the Prevention of Crimes Act (formerly the Habitual Criminals Act 1869) had been registered and photographed. This had resulted in the accumulation of a large number of names of criminals the majority of which were unlikely to be required. In consequence, the usefulness of the Registry as a means of identification was much impeded by the difficulty and loss of time involved in searching among so large a mass of names and descriptions.

To remedy this state of affairs the Register was to be restricted to two types of criminal. The first of these was the habitual criminal, that is a person convicted on indictment of a crime listed in the Prevention of Crimes Act 1871 who had a previous conviction for crime. The second was the ex-convict, that is a person discharged from a sentence of penal servitude after a conviction for crime. This demarcation continued in place up to and following the re-transfer in 1896 of the Habitual Criminals Register back from the Home Office to the Commissioner of the Metropolis.

Criminal records below the national level

Although the Metropolitan Police served a national function it was also the headquarters of the largest police force in the country. Although it had been suggested from time to time, it would have been wasteful for the Metropolitan Police to maintain separate registers for itself and for the country as a whole and so one set of Metropolitan Police files and indexes was used for both national and Metropolitan Police purposes. The principal records used in this way were the finger-print collection, the photographs of criminals, the files relating to criminals, and the name index to these files.

Police forces have, of course, always had the right to keep such records as were necessary to perform their duties. To some extent the need for records depends on the size of the force, but one of the criticisms made of the smaller forces was that they were too small to be able to afford specialist officers. This was particularly true of the smaller city and borough forces.

West Riding Modus Operandi Classification Department

On 6 July 1908 Major L.W. Atcherley became Chief Constable of the West Riding Constabulary. Under his leadership a number of innovations to the local criminal record system were introduced. In 1913 Atcherley published a book with the title 'M.O.' (Modus Operandi). This provided details of the system he had developed for reporting and identifying particular crimes which showed any distinctive character. His new Modus Operandi Crime Classification Department at the Wakefield headquarters soon became of interest to neighbouring forces, and the West Riding headquarters became known as the Clearing House of the North.

The Home Office were interested in Atcherley's approach and in July 1913 it was the main item on the agenda of a sub-committee of the Chief Constables' Club. This reported in favour of extending the system with clearing houses (criminal record offices at Scotland Yard covering central and southern

England, at Birmingham covering the Midlands and at Wakefield covering Northern England. It recommended Scotland Yard to be the co-ordinating authority with the title 'Central Criminal Record Office'. The Home Office Inspectors of Constabulary were in favour of the clearing house system.

The Commissioner's counter proposals

To some extent the recommendations of the Chief Constables' Club were a recognition of the personal attitudes taken up by the various chief constables involved, for the West Riding was not going to give up its clearing house, Birmingham was determined to set one up and the Metropolitan Police considered that their function was the oversight of the whole country's records. Such a reconciliation of interests proved to be fragile because ultimately the Commissioner did not support it. On 23 September 1913 the Commissioner wrote to the Home Office referring to the work of the sub-committee of the Chief Constables' Club. He alleged that the original proposal was that the Metropolitan Police should act as a Clearing House for the whole of England and Wales but that because of Wakefield's and Birmingham's determination to have their own registries the sub-committee had suggested that these be officially recognised. He admitted that police practice hitherto had been defective as regards the travelling criminal because only serious cases found their way into the *Police Gazette* and that in minor cases all that was done was to circulate lists of stolen property by 'routes'. Such circulations were of little value without the complete information which might enable other forces to recognize the criminal from the similarity of his methods. The Wakefield system was to keep special records of the movement of thieves who could be identified by their methods and crimes according to their methods. The Commissioner claimed that the classification of criminals by the methods peculiar to them had begun in London some time before with useful results. What was new in the Wakefield scheme was to do this in the provinces and to arrange intercommunication between provincial detective officers.

The Commissioner argued that the establishment of local records offices was a retrograde step. The information was already available in the Criminal Record Office and it was wasteful to employ staff to duplicate records and to classify them locally. He also said that there was a danger that public confidence in the fingerprint system could be shaken by faulty identification. Since it was not possible for a local Clearing House to guarantee that their record of an offender included all offences committed in all parts of the country, there was a danger that incomplete criminal records could be placed before the Court and of the offender obtaining, say, probation rather than a substantial sentence. The

Commissioner said that no decentralised Criminal Record Office could be efficient as a protection against the travelling criminal.

He further claimed that although the counties of Derbyshire, Durham, East Riding, Lancashire, North Riding and Nottinghamshire, the boroughs of Durham, Middlesborough and Newcastle and all the boroughs in Lancashire and Yorkshire except Manchester had combined with West Riding, a number of police forces in the North continued to obtain information from Scotland Yard. He recommended as an alternative to the sub-committee's proposals a number of measures to improve the method of communicating information about travelling criminals which would adopt the useful features of Atcherley's method and make Scotland Yard central registry indispensable to all forces irrespective of whether or not they maintained their own local registry.

Although there were improvements to the issuing of the Police Gazette, the substance of the controversy and the Commissioner's proposals lay dormant for the duration of the First World War.

After the war the Home Office again took up the question of regional clearing houses. It established a conference panel to visit West Riding and Scotland Yard. The report of the panel noted that the methods used by the Metropolitan Police and the West Riding Constabulary were manifestly different, particularly as regards the modus operandi classification system, and it was suggested that experts from both forces devise a common system. As regards the number of clearing houses, the conference left open the need for a third clearing house in Birmingham.

The conclusions were not acceptable to the Commissioner and an acrimonious exchange of letters ensued. Eventually, the Home Office decided that in view of the Commissioner's unco-operative attitude it would be useless to attempt to make any sort of progress at that time. On the other hand it was not going to comply with the Commissioner's request that Wakefield should limit its activities to the West Riding. On 26 April 1922 it issued a circular to police authorities and chief constables suggesting the basis on which the cost of the West Riding scheme should be shared among forces already using the Wakefield Clearing House or who might later decide to participate in it. No further action on the matter of clearing houses was taken by the Home Office until 1933 when it set up the Departmental Committee on Detective Work and Procedure.

Trenchard's changes 1934

On 25 January 1934, when Lord Trenchard had become Metropolitan Police Commissioner, Trenchard wrote to the Home Office suggesting a number of changes to improve the fingerprints and criminal record system. He proposed, inter alia, that the Fingerprint Office should have its own Name Index of Criminals. Whereas this was bound to some extent to duplicate the Nominal Index in the Criminal Record Office it would contain details of fingerprint classification and would avoid the need for both fingerprint and Criminal Record Office staff attempting to search the same index at the same time. Trenchard also proposed that the property index which had just been set up be extended and that the Method Index which was now regarded as the backbone of the Criminal Record Office be brought up to date – it was 7 months in arrear.

Departmental Committee on Detective Work and Procedure 1933-38

The Home Office Departmental Committee sat from 1933 to 1938 and carried out a survey of police records in England and Wales which was one of the most thorough ever made. It divided itself into a number of sub-committees each specialising in a particular subject. Whilst recognising that there was a need for local police records the 1938 Report pointed out that not even the largest force could be self contained in crime matters and that existing local police systems were subject to some inherent disadvantages whenever police action was needed to be applied to a common purpose over a wide area. The Committee argued that whereas co-operative arrangements had been much extended and improved in many ways in the preceding years, much still needed to be done to develop systematic co-operation in the fields of detective work and organization.

The Committee noted that there were striking variations in the form, range and organisation of the records in the individual forces, particularly in the records of criminals. While the Committee believed that the maintenance of records of local criminals was an essential part of the detective organisation of every force and that local initiative should not be unduly cramped, it felt that the requirements of the different forces were identical in principle and that it was desirable that local records should be framed on a common plan. This plan should be suitable for use in systems serving the needs both of individual forces and of regional and national areas. The Committee argued that although each force must keep its records of local criminals, any system for the registration of convicted prisoners must be national in scope, should be based on the Henry fingerprint system and should be kept by the Metropolitan Police. It thus endorsed the then existing central criminal record system. The Committee accepted that all forces should keep photographs of travelling criminals but it felt that there was a need for records of such offenders to be held at a centre serving a wider geographical area than a single force. This raised the issues of whether there should be regional offices or whether a single central office could suffice and what form the records should take. The sub-committee dealing with these issues was sharply divided and the situation was not helped by various newspaper articles in 1934 which had acclaimed the achievements of certain county and borough forces.

In July 1936 the Metropolitan Police issued to chief constables a pamphlet entitled 'Catching Thieves on Paper'. This was a useful description of the work of the Criminal Record Office at Scotland Yard but the Home Office felt its issue at a time when the committee had not yet put forward its proposals was liable to mislead any chief constable who was thinking of setting up his own force record system. The Home Office thereupon wrote to all chief constables advising them to await the committee's report.

The sub-committee working on the problem of whether the Scotland Yard or West Riding form of criminal indexes should be adopted as the standard were unable to decide the issue. In the end the Chairman and the Secretary of the main committee produced a scheme which combined from both systems the features which seemed most practical to them. The main committee agreed to recommend this scheme.

The scheme was circulated to chief constables in January 1937 in advance of the report of the committee. They were advised that they could set up or revise their existing records on the basis of the scheme. The circular gave specifications and samples of a complete range of indexes for use.

As regards the issue of central versus regional clearing houses, the 1938 Report accepted that it was not always practicable for forces to obtain information from Scotland Yard as speedily as was necessary for crime detection purposes. The Committee noted that the Wakefield Clearing House had been of benefit not only to the West Riding Constabulary but to a range of neighbouring forces. The Committee recommended that similar clearing houses be set up at Bristol for South West England, at Birmingham for the Midlands, at Cardiff for South Wales and at Liverpool for North Wales and the North West of England.

The types of records to be held at the proposed clearing houses and at Wakefield were single fingerprints; criminals' files; photographs and name indexes; modus operandi index. The Committee emphasised that these regional offices were to be clearing houses and not criminal record offices. They were to be 'live' offices for crime detection purposes, but should not attempt to usurp the role of the Central Criminal Record Office at Scotland Yard by seeking to establish a full record of convictions of those from outside their geographical area.

The proposals were discussed in July 1939 at the first meeting of the Advisory Committee on Police Regional Services. It was agreed that a regional scheme should be prepared. The outbreak of war in 1939 meant that once again the matter of regional clearing houses had to be put aside.

Working Party on Crime Classification and Clearing Houses 1949-52

It must be remembered that prior to the 1964 Police Act the Home Office's ability to influence individual chief constables was limited; its principle weapon was persuasion. In consequence, in the absence of legislation the co-operation of the individual forces was the only way that the Departmental Committee's recommendations could be implemented. To secure this co-operation, the Home Office appointed a Working Party of chief constables in January 1949 to examine the recommendations. The Working Party's report was issued in 1952. It endorsed most of the recommendations but also made some alternative proposals.

The Working Party agreed that there could be only one national criminal record office for England and Wales and pointed out that this was endorsed by section 39 of the 1948 Criminal Justice Act which provided that a statement of previous convictions certified by the Commissioner of Police of the Metropolis to contain particulars relating to convictions extracted from the records kept by him was to be accepted by the courts as prima facie evidence of such convictions. It agreed that the term national was inappropriate for the Scotland Yard Criminal Record Office (given the offices in Scotland and Northern Ireland) and recommended that it be known as the Central Criminal Record Office.

The Working Party agreed that there was a need for regional offices but did not consider the term 'Clearing House' was entirely suitable for describing the centres where criminal records were housed and recommended that they be called Regional Criminal Record Offices.

The recommendations of the Working Party were implemented slowly. By 1966, however, the regional offices had been established:

> Midland Criminal Record Office
> West Riding Criminal Record Office
> North Eastern Criminal Record Office
> Merseyside Criminal Record Office
> Manchester Criminal Record Office
> Lancashire Criminal Record Office
> Western Criminal Record Office
> South Western Criminal Record Office
> Southern Group Criminal Record Office

Throughout the 1970s policy matters on criminal records were dealt with under the Standing Committee on Criminal Record Offices, chaired by Her Majesty's Inspector of Constabulary (Crime), representing the Home Office, and consisted of chief constables responsible for the operation of the regional offices and representatives of the Scottish and Northern Ireland offices and the Central Criminal Record Office.

The development of criminal records in the USA

In a democratic society composed of millions of citizens, identifying those who have a criminal background in order to allocate social punishment poses unique problems. In the United States, these problems were complicated by the fact that, from the beginning, there was no national police force, criminal justice functions were allocated largely to the states and localities by the Constitution. Second, the USA, at the turn of the century was itself a society of strangers. In some northeastern cities, more than 30 per cent of the population were immigrants, most of whom did not even speak the same language as the police and judicial authorities. Third, the USA differed from Europe in that there was no centralized national registry of citizens similar to those in the Napoleonic code countries, nor were there restrictions or records on the mobility of citizens. The first modern criminal history systems emerged in the northeastern cities in the 1890's (Marchand 1980). Various states established bureaus of criminal identification and statistics to act as depositories for arrest records throughout the state and as clearinghouses for information about offenders from other states and jurisdictions. In 1896, New York became the first state to establish a bureau of criminal identification. As part of the prison department, the State Bureau of Criminal Identification was authorized by law to procure and file *Bertillon* measurements of all prisoners confined or admitted to state prisons, reformatories, and penitentiaries. In 1903, the Bureau began filing fingerprints of inmates of state prisons. Both systems of identification were used until, in 1913, fingerprinting was required by law for all inmates of the state prisons, reformatories and penitentiaries. A Central Bureau of Criminal Identification was established in 1927 as a division in the Department of Correction, which had replaced the Prison Department. In 1928, a state law was passed requiring all law enforcement agencies in the state to fingerprint all persons arrested and charged with a felony or misdemeanour. In addition, it required that a copy of each set of prints be forwarded to the Division of Criminal Identification, Records and Statistics, in the state capital.

In 1954, the Division was separated into the Division of Criminal Identification and the Division of Research. Then, in 1957, to acknowledge the annual receipt of more non-criminal than criminal fingerprints, the word criminal was dropped from the title of the Division of Criminal Identification. The Division of Identification operated a manual information system that collected and disseminated arrest records and criminal history records throughout the state of New York until 1966, when it was transferred to the New York State Identification and Intelligence System (NYSIIS). The criminal files were subsequently computerized.

A similar pattern of development occurred in California, where the Bureau of Criminal Identification was established in 1905 in San Quentin Prison (Kenney 1964). Its primary purpose was to fingerprint inmates and to distribute copies of prints to major police departments in California for use in identifying subjects who might be arrested again at some future time. In 1917, after much political activity by law enforcement agencies throughout the state, a Bureau of Criminal Identification and Investigation was created under state law. The statute established categories, for arrested persons whose fingerprints were to be submitted to the bureau and described what reports on major crimes and stolen, lost property were to be submitted by local police departments.

In 1929 a statistical function was added to the bureau, based on the recommendations of the California Crime Commission. In 1941, the bureau was integrated into the Department of Justice; when the Department was reorganised in 1951, the bureau was placed under the Division of Criminal Law and Enforcement. The Bureau of Criminal Statistics, created in 1955 by the legislature, was responsible for processing information relating to police, probation and court activities. By the late 1960s, the Bureau of Criminal Identification and Investigation had computerized a portion of its records which had been maintained manually since 1918.

By 1965, 42 states had developed central record keeping systems for criminal offenders. The systems varied widely, but three basic files generally were maintained: fingerprinting, name index to prints, and criminal history records (Bratt 1970).

The FBI's dominating presence

In 1924, the Federal Bureau of Investigation (FBI) was established as the only clearinghouse for 'criminal identification records'. Prior to this time the function of collecting, maintaining, and disseminating such information as fingerprints, photographs, and criminal histories of offenders on a national scale was performed by the Central Bureau of Identification at the Federal Penitentiary at Fort Leavenworth, and by the National Bureau of Criminal Identification operated by the International Association of Chiefs of Police (IACP), a private organization based in Washington, DC.

In 1923, the International Association of Chiefs of Police offered to turn over their fingerprint files to the Department of Justice, provided that the Department would establish a central criminal bureau in Washington, DC, which would carry on the services to police throughout the USA. The offer was taken up and the FBI Identification Division was established. In 1929, the then Director, J. Edgar Hoover was successful in making the Identification Division a permanent part of the FBI by congressional authority. Kenneth Laudon concludes that:

> "Hoover's Identification Division – the nation's first national criminal history system - was established in an atmosphere characterized, if not by hysteria, then by shock and disappointment that crime had become so widespread and threatening in America. And criminal history record systems were proffered by professional police groups and the federal government as one technologically sophisticated way of coping with this new insecurity".   (Laudon 1986: 35)

The Identification Division collected fingerprint and arrest records submitted by local, state, and federal law enforcement agencies for crimes serious enough to require taking prints. The cumulative record of an individual's arrests, dispositions, and sentences comprises what the FBI calls a criminal history record or rap sheet. An example of the manual record (from Marchand 1980: 118) is shown in figure 3.

In 1965, following the major urban riots which took place across the USA, Congress passed the Law Enforcement Assistance Act of 1965. The law was a hastily drawn up statute, with an emphasis upon improving the ability of local law enforcement agencies to restore and maintain law and order in the cities. The program established by the law was to provide federal funds, primarily to local police, for training personnel and for equipment. Some funds appropriated by the Act were used to support the work of the Presidential Commission whose job it was to conduct an in-depth study of law enforcement and criminal justice and develop longer term solutions. As an interim measure, the 1965 Act was given a limited lifespan of only three years, with an accompanying appropriation of $ 10 million for each year.

Co-incidentally, in 1965 the computer industry first introduced its 'third generation' computer systems (e.g. IBM 360 series). These new computers produced a virtual revolution in the application of computer technology. They made possible, for the first time, large-scale information systems which combined computers and communications systems to allow large and complex computer data-bases to be accessible for storage and retrieval of information

Figure 3

UNITED STATES DEPARTMENT OF JUSTICE
Federal Bureau of Investigation
Identification Division
Washington, D.C. 20537
Fictitious Record

The following FBI record, NUMBER 000 000 X, is furnished FOR OFFICIAL USE ONLY. Information shown on this Identification Record represents data furnished to FBI by fingerprint contributors. WHERE DISPOSITION IS NOT SHOWN OR FURTHER EXPLANATION OF CHARGE OR DISPOSITION IS DESIRED, COMMUNICATE WITH AGENCY CONTRIBUTING THOSE FINGERPRINTS.

Contributor of Fingerprints	Name and Number	Arrested or Received	Charge	Disposition
SO Clanton AL	John Doe A-000	3-9-65	susp	rel
SO Clanton AL	John J.Doe A-000	6-11-65	vag	rel
SO Clanton AL	John J.Doe A-000	9-18-65	intox	$25 or 25 days; pd
PD Montgomery AL	Joseph Doe CC-000	6-11-66	forg	
St Bd of Corr Montgomery AL	John Joseph Doe C-00000	10-18-66	forg 2nd deg	2 yrs & 1 day par 5-15-67
St Bd of Corr Montgomery AL	Joseph John Doe C-00000	returned 9-5-67	PV (forg 2nd deg)	to serve unexpired term of 2yrs & 1 day
PD Montgomery AL	John Doe A-0000	2-20-68	burg & escapee	TOT St Bd of Corr Montgomery AL
St Bd of Corr Montgomery AL	John J Doe C-00000	returned 2-21-68	burg & escapee	2 yrs
USM Jacksonville FL	John J Doe 00-C	10-14-70	ITSMV	

from an almost unlimited number of remote 'sites', which could be scattered throughout the country.

Diana Gordon describes the political background to these developments:

"As the federal planners saw it, the challenge of modern criminality could be met only with a flexing of national muscle. Over and over, reports of the President's Commission on Law Enforcement and Criminal Justice formed in 1965 emphasised the need for supplementing traditional state and local crime control activities with federal research, federal experiments, and federal money...Federal coordination could best be achieved by such Commission proposals as the creation of 'a central computerized office into which each federal agency would feed all of its organized crime intelligence'. The Commission's Task Force on Science and Technology went farther, recommending 'an integrated national information system' for courts and corrections, as well as police, a computerized network that would ultimately link law enforcement activities of all kinds at all levels of government".   (Gordon 1990: 55)

Even prior to some of these developments, the FBI quickly seized upon the new technology and proposed the establishment of a major new system for supplying criminal information to police nationwide. The system proposed was called the National Crime Information Centre (NCIC), which would be established within the Identification Division. In October 1966, the concept of NCIC was adopted by the International Association of Chiefs of Police.

The technology, the national concern for law and order, and the Law Enforcement Assistance Act of 1965 all combined to create an irresistible climate for the creation of the NCIC. As a result, the NCIC program became the single largest program funded under the 1965 Act, receiving approximately $800,000 of the total $30,000,000 appropriated by the Act for years 1966-68 (Zenk 1979).

Following computerization of around 195,000 federal offenders' criminal history files, in 1966 the Attorney General approved FBI proposals to establish the NCIC that would develop computerized criminal information systems. In July 1967, the NCIC became operational with five files in its computer data base: persons wanted by the police for extraditable offences, and assorted stolen property files. Criminal histories, or 'rap sheets', were not included in the data base at that time. Fifteen state and local law enforcement agencies across the nation were linked to the NCIC through the NCIC's own communications network. Each of these control terminals could, in turn, to tied to additional agencies through their own local and state networks. In addition, the NCIC was also linked of course to FBI offices throughout the country. The type of information supplied by NCIC was of little interest to criminal justice agencies other than law enforcement. It was geared to supplying the policeman in the field with information which would help him make operational decisions. However, by 1968 NCIC began to make plans for the inclusion of computerized criminal history records. In evidence to the Ervin Committee in 1974, the basis of these early plans is retold by the FBI:

> " In September 1968, NCIC staff (and Working Committee Members) met to discuss standards, procedures and policies for a CCH (computerized criminal history) file. At this meeting a prototype criminal history summary and a complete criminal history record were examined for the first time. By February 1969, the basic offense classification standards were established. To facilitate the development of CCH, the FBI contacted the Law Enforcement Assistance Administration in the spring of 1969, with the idea of forming a group of advanced computer states with mandatory reporting laws to demonstrate an interstate exchange of criminal history. Five states were recommended, and LEAA sponsored Project SEARCH...The purpose of this project was to demonstrate the feasibility of exchanging criminal history data interstate by means of a computerized system." (U.S. Congress, Senate 1974: 661).

The history of what followed next in the period 1968 till the early 1980s' is analysed by several commentators (see Zenk 1979; Marchand 1980; Laudon 1986). In some ways, the policy debate in this period on a national criminal history record rivals Greek mythology, both in terms of the number of actors involved and the diversity of activities in which they engaged. What is clear, to use Downs' terminology (Downs 1967), is that in 1968 the FBI occupied virtually all the 'policy space' in the field of national criminal information systems. This was rapidly to change.

Enter Project SEARCH

The Omnibus Crime Control and Safe Streets Act of 1968 created, among other things, a new federal bureaucracy, the Law Enforcement Assistance Administration (LEAA). Concerned that the state systems which it was funding would lead to a bewildering array of independent and incompatible systems that would not be able to share information, it has been suggested that the LEAA began an initiative known as Project SEARCH (System for the Electronic Analysis and Retrieval of Criminal History Records) in 1968. However, there is no consensus on the origins of SEARCH. Zenk (1979: 114) is of the view that the evidence by the FBI to Congress in 1974 (quoted above) is probably closer to the truth. Zenk continues:

"There is obviously some irony...the FBI probably was responsible for suggesting Project SEARCH in the first instance. But the FBI at that time was thinking only of a limited project to test the feasibility of its own concept for expanding the National Crime Information Centre capabilities to include computerized FBI 'rap sheets'. It is quite possible that, in 1969, the FBI could have quite easily conducted this pilot project itself and implemented the new service as routinely as it introduced other NCIC computer applications. However, at the time, the FBI saw the new LEAA program as an opportunity to promote its own ends rather than as a challenge to its domination of the field of criminal information systems at the national level. And there was little in the FBI's experience up to that time to suggest that it was in fact taking an unusual risk".

(Zenk ibid: 115)

Project SEARCH, initially presented as a fourteen-month pilot project, had two very specific aims (Project SEARCH, 1970):

(a) to establish and demonstrate the feasibility of an on-line system allowing for the interstate exchange of offender files in the states based on a compatible "criminal justice offender record", integrating police, prosecution, court and correctional offender data

(b) design and demonstrate a computerized criminal justice statistics system which would permit access by the LEAA and police, court and correctional agencies.

Zenk in his important study attempts to explain why and how Project SEARCH evolved from a six state project into a permanent organization of all fifty states. He focuses on the role which the Project played in the developing political relationships between states and the federal government on the one hand, and between two competing federal bureaucracies, the LEAA and the FBI, on the other.

In essence, Project SEARCH proved that use of a computerized system for the interstate exchange of criminal histories was technically feasible. The next questions concerned who should operate the system and what computerized criminal history information should be maintained at the federal and state levels. During the summer of 1970, the Office of the Attorney General, the FBI, and the LEAA discussed possible alternatives. Essentially there were five:

Alternative 1	One state could operate a central index
Alternative 2	A consortium of states could operate the central index
Alternative 3	The FBI could operate the central index as part of its NCIC
Alternative 4	LEAA could operate the central index as part of its information services to the states
Alternative 5	A joint LEAA/FBI computer facility could operate the central index

The first alternative, that one state would operate the index, was rejected by both the FBI and LEAA. Although this alternative would ensure that the system would be controlled by the states, it had substantial disadvantages: first, it singled out one state to provide what is essentially a national service, and there would be a continual possibility of legislative changes that could affect the program. Second, this alternative had funding mechanism difficulties. Third, the operation of the computer would involve both state and federal functions, which would create administrative problems. Similarly, the second alternative was seen as administratively and politically overcomplicated.

Marchand, (1980) in his wide-ranging analysis of the politics of this area notes that a significant difference of opinion arose on the remaining options, three, four and five. The Director of the FBI set out three reasons why the Bureau should maintain a central index for the exchange of criminal histories with the states: first, the FBI had legal authority and past experience; second, the FBI, in operating the only nationwide criminal statistics service - the Uniform Crime Reports – had helped to set standards for local and state law enforcement agencies; third, since 1967 the NCIC had been operational and was both a computerized information system and a nationwide communications system. However, despite this line of reasoning, Marchand points out that the LEAA had their own particular agenda when considering this matter.

Zenk, (1979) points out that the initial SEARCH system concept was modelled to a large extent on the New York State Identification and Intelligence System (NYSIIS). Unlike most other state systems, NYSIIS was organizationally separated from all line law enforcement functions and was developed from the beginning to be a service to the whole criminal justice community rather than being basically a police operation.

The initial SEARCH concept adapted from the Summer 1969 pilot study was called the 'Agency of Record' :

> "This concept took the suggestion of the President's Commission on Law Enforcement and Administration of Justice for an 'integrated national criminal justice information system; based on the notion that law enforcement is primarily a local and State function', and carried it farther in the direction of state versus federal orientation".   (Zenk 1979: 24)

The SEARCH 'Agency of Record' concept, therefore, had three main components:

1. Computerized criminal history files at the state level.

2 . A central index containing identification data, a summary of arrests and convictions, and a 'pointer' to the Agency of Record holding the most up-to-date criminal history record.

3 . A communications network, including a 'message-switching' device, capable of linking state-level computers.

According to Zenk ,(1979), "By favouring the SEARCH system concept the states clearly indicated a desire to maintain direct control over criminal history information, either individually or at least collectively", (Zenk ibid: 27).

It soon became clear to the then Attorney General, John Mitchell, that the debate over who would implement SEARCH was not going to be settled. Mitchell, therefore, requested the influential Office of Management and Budget to review Project SEARCH and make recommendations. On 3 September, 1970 the Office reported on its review. There were three main recommendations:

> "a. That the SEARCH effort at the Federal level be restricted to the operation of the Central Index (limited in the amount of data contained on each criminal), and that the States develop and generate their own criminal history systems as developed in the SEARCH concept.
>
> b. That the FBI be designated to operate the SEARCH Central Index as the communication switch. This should avoid establishing a system that would completely duplicate the existing systems support.
>
> c. That a strong policy control board to make decisions on the future development and implementation of the nationwide SEARCH system should be lodged in the Office of the Attorney General, with balanced policy-vele representation from the FBI, the LEAA, and the States. This

control feature would ease the serious concerns of the States that, without strong State participation in the policy decisions, Federal operation of the Central Index could lead to an eventual expansion of the Index into a centralized national data bank. Such expansion would have serious implications for individual privacy and would intrude into the States' desire to maintain and control their own detailed criminal history files. The presentation of the States' intention in this regard is consistent with and supports the concept and spirit of the 'New Federalism".

(US Congress/Senate 1974, Criminal Justice Data Banks Vol 2: 368)

The review generally endorsed, therefore, the SEARCH approach. However, within three months of the Office of Management and Budget review, Mitchell notified the LEAA that he had decided to assign sole authority to implement an operational system for the interstate exchange of computerized criminal history files to the FBI.

Zenk (1979) in his analysis of Attorney General Mitchell's decision draws the conclusion, from available evidence, that the decision was made on the basis of expediency and political compromise, and not on the basis of any demonstration of technical feasibility.

Following Mitchell's decision in December 1970, the F.B.I. organized its efforts to implement the new criminal history system within the framework of its National Crime Information Centre (NCIC). Thus began a series of proposals and programs conducted by the FBI to develop a national computerized criminal history (CCH) system. However, both the LEAA (until its demise in 1978) and the states continued to oppose proposals of the FBI in the area of a national CCH system.

Laudon (1986) discusses in some detail the proposals of the 1970s. The early Single-State/Multistate (NCIC-CCH) system is set out in figure 4.

In this system, states would maintain single-state offender records. NCIC-CCH would include records of multistate and federal offenders. In addition, NCIC would maintain a name index of single-state offenders whose full records would be held by the states. Most importantly, NCIC would develop a sophisticated message-switching telecommunications system which would be used to direct enquiries through the NCIC computer and communication lines from the requesting state agency to the originating state. The record of interest would be transmitted to the requesting state via the NCIC network. This meant that the FBI would act as the telecommunications centre for the interstate transmission of all criminal history records in the United States. Every state request would have to go through the FBI.

However, only a handful of states ever participated fully in this program, and the majority of states objected to the proposed message switching and the

Figure 4

Single State/ Multistate CCH with Message Switching
(NCIC Original Proposal)

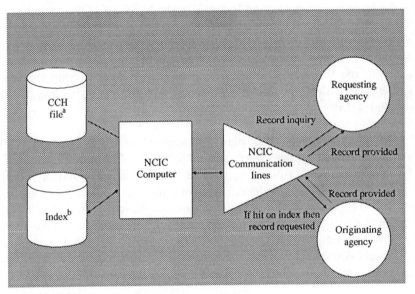

Source: Office of Technology Assessment.

Notes:
[a] For multi-State and Federal offender records.
[b] For single-State offender records located in State repositories.

need to submit and update records to a centralized file operated by the FBI. The task for the FBI was therefore :

"to decide whether a national CCH could be developed without message switching and without a centralized full-record criminal history file, but with the capacity to maintain the predominance of the FBI in a national system. It was not long before the technical staff of the FBI devised such a program".
(Laudon 1986: 66)

This new program was formally advised to the US Congress by the FBI in the early 1980s and has been developed ever since. Under the development plan of the Interstate Identification Index (III), the NCIC-CCH file includes only the records of federal offenders plus a national index of all single-state and multi-state offender records. This national index is a name index and does not require the submission by the states of complete criminal history records. In addition, the Interstate Identification Index uses existing communications systems, thus dealing with the objection of message switching. Laudon concludes that:

"In many respects, this plan is identical to the plan successfully demonstrated by the LEAA and Project SEARCH in 1969. The policy debate had come full circle, with LEAA and the states having won the conceptual battle of the development of a 'national name index', sometimes called a 'pure-pointer index system' because the federal files would simply be a name index pointing to the state that held the complete record. Unfortunately for LEAA and the states, the FBI, not LEAA or the states, would control the central national file. LEAA won the conceptual battle but ultimately lost the political and bureaucratic battle".
(Laudon ibid: 66)

In many ways, the two major issues in the development towards a national criminal record in the USA throughout the 1970s and early 1980s were – first the matter of legislative and executive control and second the issue of the constitutional limits on criminal justice information systems, for example in relation to privacy. In this brief review we have concentrated on the first issue, but we shall have more to say on matters of constitutional controls in chapter 5. Diana Gordon in her analysis of the legacy of the LEAA, succinctly presents the wider legacy of the post 1968 period:

"As the patron saint of the technological revolution in law enforcement, it had elevated the local police officer into Supercop by making state and national collections of hot files and criminal history records instantly available. And, while there were a few naysayers who doubted the crime control efficacy of criminal history networks or worried about their intrusions on privacy, the idea of a national criminal justice information system, fed by thousands of local and state databases, many of them linked to one another, had gained nearly universal acceptance in law enforcement."   (Gordon 1990: 61-2)

3 Contemporary systems

In this chapter we examine the present configuration of criminal record systems in the UK and USA. The concerns that have arisen in recent years over concepts of data quality and confidentiality are also explored, and we provide a review of the problem of 'unofficial disclosure' as a backdrop to our discussions on official disclosures from the criminal record in later chapters.

The UK

As was pointed out in chapter 2, records about a person's criminal history have long been maintained by the police primarily because this information was considered of value to the investigation and detection of crime. Before looking at the configuration of current police record and information systems in the UK, it worth noting the present legal basis.

Under the Prevention of Crimes Act of 1871, the Commissioner of Police of the Metropolis was given the responsibility of creating and maintaining a register of convicted criminals in order to "facilitate their identification". This statute, repealed by the Criminal Law Act of 1967, is of course the origin of the so-called National Collection of Criminal Records maintained by the National Identification Bureau (NIB) for the use of all police forces.

The information held has traditionally been provided also to the courts to assist in the determination of punishment following conviction, although there is no statutory obligation on the police to do so. Information is also provided to certain Government departments, local authorities and agencies and organizations for purposes ranging from the protection of children, national security and ensuring 'proper' administration of justice. Usually, this information is provided by local police forces at the discretion of individual chief constables under guidance issued from the Home Office as circulars. There are however a few situations where there does exist a statutory obligation on the police to provide criminal record information, for example - the case of prospective adoptive parents.

The National Collection of Criminal Records referred to above contains details of persons convicted of, or who are to be prosecuted for, reportable offences. These offences are broadly those which the police believe to be of sufficient interest to merit recording at a national level. They form a subset of recordable offences, whose definition is given in the 1984 Police and Criminal Evidence Act. Under S.27(4) of the 1984 Act, the "Secretary of State may make provision for recording in national police records, convictions for such offences as are specified in the regulations.". Regulations made in 1985 and 1989 define the types of convictions which may be recorded in the national records (SI No.1941, 1985; SI No. 694, 1989). The regulations state that convictions punishable with imprisonment can be recorded as well as offences under:

a.   S.1 of the Street Offences Act 1959 (loitering or soliciting for purposes of prostitution)

b.   S.43 of the Telecommunications Act 1984 (improper use of the telecommunications system)

c.   S.29 of the Road Traffic Act 1972 (tampering with motor vehicles)

d.   S.1 of the Malicious Communications Act 1988 (offence of sending letters with intent to cause distress)

e.   S.139(1) of the Criminal Justice Act 1988 (offence of having an article in a public place with blade).

However, personal information held by the police in the UK is currently maintained in various different locations. The Police National Computer (PNC) services forces throughout the UK and including the Isle of Man and the Channel Islands. The PNC holds some criminal records (those recorded since 1st January 1981) and an index to where others can be located in the NIB. The NIB, administered by the Metropolitan Police and located at New Scotland

Yard in London, holds the definitive version of the National Collection of Criminal Records. Scotland and Northern Ireland have their own criminal record offices. Some local police forces keep their own criminal record offices as well as storing more speculative criminal intelligence. At the national level, a beginning has been made on the establishment of a National Criminal Intelligence Service (NCIS).

The Police National Computer

The inauguration of the PNC in 1974 represented the outcome of discussions between the Home Office and the police that started in the early 1960s. Physically located in Hendon, North London, the PNC offered a computerized information service on crime and criminals that could be accessed by police forces throughout the country. The computer software was developed internally by the Home Office and the police. By 1985 preparations were being made to upgrade the PNC (see Campbell & Connor 1986 for the background to this). The PNC upgrading was to counter the escalating costs of hardware maintenance that were then running at £ 1 million pounds per annum, and to also try and reduce the 350 staff required to operate it. These specific objectives were within the broader context of attempting to gain "not only more computer power, but also greater efficiency and flexibility to develop advanced applications" (Wasserman 1989). To replace the 'home-grown' software, the regrading involved private tendering, and Software AG won the contract offering the ADABAS database and NATURAL programming language. Processing is provided by a new Siemens 7.500 mainframe computer (Wasserman 1989).

The upgrade referred to as PNC2, came on-line in November 1991, but has overlap functions from the original PNC1. The new PNC2 capacity has over 190 million bytes of data on its main memory and 80,000 million bytes on disk. The databases and number of entries on the PNC2 are:

" - vehicles (including stolen reports) 40,270,232
- persons (includes wanted/missing/disqualified drivers) 5,614,247
- convictions 4,036,366
- fingerprints 4,333,495
- stolen property 39,399
- police directories 3,542 " (Hansard 23 January 1992 col 319)

Certain applications remain on the PNC1 equipment but are not in general use by the police. These include the extremist crime index and crime pattern analysis. However, recent Government statements point out that the aim is to take the PNC1 out of service as soon as possible.

Using secure private circuits leased from British Telecom, the PNC2 has lines to 2,600 terminals across the UK, and some 41 standard interface arrangements to local police computer systems. An average 8,000 inquiries an hour are handled on the PNC2 and some 100,000 per day. The PNC2 is managed directly by the Home Office as a Common Police Service funded 51 per cent by the Home Office and 49 per cent by local police authorities. Operational use is derived solely by the local forces using it, and they, in turn, are represented on the Police National Computer Organization which is chaired by a Home Office official, and meets quarterly. Training for staff operating the PNC2 is carried out at their own training unit in Durham.

The PNC2 criminal names index is the first port of call for a police officer wishing to identify the criminal history of a person. The index identifies whether or not a person has a record and gives the officer a criminal record reference number (CRO no.) for use to check via the NIB. The criminal names index contains no criminal records in itself, but serves as the pointer to further information held at the NIB.

The conviction history index contains names and details of reportable convictions since 1981. It does not contain the more detailed information available from the NIB. It may be sufficient for many police purposes, but in most instances a full search of the definitive national collection of criminal records at the NIB may be necessary. The PNC is subject to the Data Protection Act 1984, which requires registration of use of such computer systems (see chapter 5).

The National Identification Bureau

The NIB has its origins in the old national Criminal Record Office at New Scotland Yard. Emerging as the NIB in 1980, the Bureau now consists of two sections – the National Fingerprint Office (NFO) and the National Criminal Record Office (NCRO) and holds the definitive record of criminal convictions for reportable offences and well as those for whom prosecution is pending. The main functions of the NIB are to provide the UK police forces with:

- confirmation of the identity of arrested persons through the matching of fingerprints
- details of previous convictions of arrested persons

- details of previous convictions of those appearing in court
- the supply of antecedent histories for investigative purposes.

The Bureau is located on the third floor of New Scotland Yard and its information is currently maintained on microfiche (having been on manual card-sort until 1982). The microfiche is a much reduced photograph of a document (see below) which is read through a special enlarging machine. Each NIB microfiche file is given a criminal record reference number (CRO No.) based on the year in which it was opened and on the number of files opened that year. There are presently microfiche records on some 5.5 million people, and the Bureau deals with in excess of 1.8 million requests a year (see House of Commons 1990a), mostly by mail but with a facility for telephone enquiry in urgent cases.

The CRO No. is entered, by the NIB, on to the PNC2 criminal names index and a brief account of convictions entered on the criminal history index. The Bureau microfiche file contains more detailed descriptions of the person, methods of committing the crime, and fingerprints and photographs if available. The system appears to be highly labour intensive and 'low-tech' compared to other systems – with row upon row of metal filing cabinets full of microfiches, and staff individually sorting the microfiche rows for insertion into the microfiche jacket or envelope.

A police officer requiring information from the NIB has first to check the PNC2 to obtain a CRO No. – if one is available. If it is, then that number is entered on the initiating form NIB 74A (see figure 5) which is delivered to NIB. Even if the number is unavailable, a negative result having been obtained on PNC2, the NIB 74A will be submitted. Detailed instructions on how to complete the form are contained in the associated form NIB 74F which also carries the warning that badly completed forms will be returned unanswered. NIB 74F also explains some of the so-called 'warning' signals shown on a PNC2 check. Warnings include the abbreviation "mental" meaning the person may suffer from a mental disorder; "M/impers" or "F/impers" that they may impersonate a man or woman, and "alleges" that they make false allegations against the police (see Home Office 1991: Annex C).

The NIB 74A includes a carbon copy of its initial information concerning a person arrested or summonsed and liable for prosecution. On the reverse side of the carbon copy is the NIB 74B (Result) (see figure 6). The NIB 74A has fingerprints attached to it as well as the CRO No. if available from the PNC2. The NIB 74A is linked up to existing records in the Master Record of the File library and checked to see if it is correct, complete and suitable for conversion to microfiche. The NIB 74A is then split to enable the top copy to be filmed for the microfiche and added to the Master Record by the jacketing section,

Figure 5

N.I.B. 74A (Arrest/Summons)   See Form N.I.B. 74F—Instructions for Completion

Fingerprints identical with .... C.R.O. No.	Fingerprint Search Negative allocated C.R.O. No.	FOR USE IN N.I.B. ONLY

Surname (CAPITALS)   Forenames

1. File Name (as shown on P.N.C.)

2. Name in which *Charged/Summonsed

3. Maiden Name (if not on P.N.C.)   4. Date of birth   5. Sex
6. Place of birth

7. Height   8. Ethnic appearance   9. Nationality

10. Build   11. Weight   12. Accent

13. Eye colour   14. Eyebrows   15. Voice

16. Hair (colour)   17. Hair (description)

18. Hair (facial)

19. Marks/Scars/Abnormalities

20. Dress

21. Details of identity documents

22. Occupation

23. Address

P.N.C. C.N. SEARCH—MUST be carried out. If subject identified enter C.R.O. No. If no trace enter N/T. If unable to identify, e.g. because of the number of responses, enter 'NOT IDENTIFIED'.   C.N. Result

Show details of P.N.C. Warning Signals	Indicate Warning Signals which are evident but NOT shown on P.N.C.
Show any changes/additions to descriptive details required to be noted on P.N.C.	FINGERPRINTS TAKEN *YES/NO PHOTOGRAPH TAKEN *YES/NO

24. *Arrested/Summonsed   *a.m./p.m. on   Charged on   *IN CUSTODY/ON BAIL

25. Appearing at   Court on

    for offence(s)

26. Method(s) used

27. Date and time of Offence   28. Location of Offence

29. Other useful information   30. Crime Ref. No.

Force Stn. Code	Arresting Officer	Tele. No.
Force	Station	Div.
Reply to be sent to (if different from above)	Supervising Officer (Name and signature)	Date

*Delete as appropriate

N.I.B. 74A

Figure 6

N.I.B. 74B (Result)

See Form N.I.B. 74F—Instruction for completion

1. C.R.O. No.

2. File Name

3. Name in which convicted

4. Aliases

5. Force/Station code

6. Nickname(s)

7. Crime Ref. No.

8. Since arrest was subject on bail   YES/NO*

9. If on bail were other offences committed   YES/NO*

10. Photograph TAKEN/NOT TAKEN*
Held at (Force/Station Code)

11. Fingerprints TAKEN/NOT TAKEN*

12. Date of sentence

13. Court

14. Offences	15. Offence Code	16. G/NG	17. Disposal
	.	. .	
	.	. .	
	.	. .	
	.	. .	
	.	. .	
	.	. .	
	.	. .	
	.	. .	
	.	. .	
	.	. .	
	.	. .	
	.	. .	
	.	. .	
	.	. .	
	.	. .	
	.	. .	
	.	. .	
	.	. .	
	.	. .	
	.	. .	
	.	. .	
	.	. .	
	.	. .	
	.	. .	
	.	. .	

(Use N.I.B. 74BB Result Continuation Form if necessary)

18. Additional information

19. Offences committed in company with

20. Police officers present at court

21. Officer in case

22. Supervising officer
(name and signature)

23. Date N.I.B. 74B completed

*delete as appropriate
M.P.83(E)

N.I.B. 74B

and also sent to the NIB's office in Croydon to be entered on the PNC convictions history index. The carbon copy of the NIB74A is returned to the force concerned along with a copy of the relevant papers from the Master Record.

After a court decision, the NIB 74B(Result) form which is on the carbon copy of NIB 74A, is completed and returned to the NIB to update the Master Record. A copy again goes to Croydon to update the PNC2 as appropriate. Where the court has dismissed a case and the person was a first offender, all records are destroyed, the PNC2 amended and fingerprints also destroyed. If the case is dismissed but the person is already on record for a previous conviction, then the record is amended accordingly.

The NIB provides a service to England and Wales with Scottish police forces being served by the Scottish Criminal Record Office in Glasgow, and in the case of Northern Ireland, the Royal Ulster Constabulary with their own office.

Staff at the NIB also continue the practice of producing the *Police Gazette* twice weekly, for circulation within police forces. The *Gazette* contains information on people wanted or missing and also includes photographs.

On current information, the NIB operates at a cost of £15-16 million pounds per annum, and with a staff of just under 700 people. Responsibility for effectiveness and efficiency rests with the Commissioner of the Metropolis.

Local record systems

Twenty nine of the forty three police forces in England and Wales have criminal record offices of their own. Of these, 25 are duplicating the records stored in the NIB, whilst the others are storing non-reportable offences which fall below the threshold deemed appropriate. All forces keep their own records of juvenile and adult cautions which they have formally administered (see chapter 4).

Local record systems are almost all manual systems based on the card index. Some larger metropolitan forces, like Greater Manchester have computerized the system. At a further level of decentralization, police divisions and sub-divisions deploy officers and civilians as collators - to record information on local crime, criminals and suspects. This information is essentially 'soft' intelligence material rather than 'hard' verified information and has in the past been criticized for its alleged excessive and sometimes prejudicial content (see Campbell 1980: 117-131 for an early critique). Collators are required to keep information up to date and to occasionally produce local bulletins for other police who in turn are encouraged to continuously submit information to the collator's office (Smith & Gray 1983: 40).

The National Criminal Intelligence Service (NCIS)

The distinction between 'soft' intelligence and the 'hard' police information systems has now become focused by the creation of the National Criminal Intelligence Service, which became operational in April 1992. The concept of a national police intelligence agency had been discussed in police circles "for 20 years" and finally came to fruition in developments in the late 1980s (Mason 1992 ; see also Fraser 1980: 230). In September 1989, the then Home Secretary Douglas Hurd, made it clear that, although he could not constitutionally impose any national organization on policing, he was not averse to others starting the discussion. Hurd also linked such developments directly to the forthcoming single-market and closer European unity post-1992 (Carvel 1989). By January 1990, an Association of Chief Police Officers working party was established to draw up proposals and consider the exact nature of this new agency (Kirby 1990).

The remit of NCIS is to:

"gather, collate, evaluate, analyze, develop, and disseminate relevant information and intelligence about serious crime and major criminals of a regional, national and international nature in order to assist and promote the efficient and effective use of operational resources and so enable the development of law enforcement strategies. To coordinate other nominated national intelligence functions".   (Home Office 1992)

In order to achieve this purpose, NCIS' structure has been formed through the amalgamation of numerous existing intelligence units. Most of these units, created in an 'ad hoc' fashion over the last decade, have had their functions subsumed by NCIS. Included in this list are:

- national drugs intelligence unit
- national football intelligence unit
- national central bureau (INTERPOL)
- public sector corruption unit
- national paedophile index
- product contamination index
- resident informants index
- commercial fraud index
- national office for the suppression of counterfeit currency
- arts and antiques squad.

In terms of its priorities, NCIS' offence list has been stated as:

- murder and attempted murder
- kidnapping, abduction and attempts
- blackmail, including extortion
- serious sexual offences
- robbery
- all offences at banks, building societies and post offices
- significant offences using firearms or imitations
- attacks on security or post office vehicles
- burglary which is aggravated
- theft of high value loads
- serious or organized fraud
- counterfeit currency and forgery
- heavy goods vehicles or machinery plant offences of special significance.

Working to an initial budget of £ 25 million, NCIS has a staff of 400, deployed in 5 regional offices in London, Manchester, Wakefield, Bristol and Birmingham. The first NCIS Director is Mr. Tony Mullett, former chief constable of West Mercia, appointed by the Home Secretary and answerable to that office. NCIS is considered a 'Common Police Service' and funded as such.

A resources committee has been established to consider NCIS finance, expenditure and staffing and the committee is composed of representatives of the Home Office, ACPO and the local police authorities. The committee has no responsibility for operational activities which are a matter solely for the Director and his management team. The Director also reports to a Standing Committee of senior police officers and civil servants from the Home Office. While NCIS is clearly an 'intelligence' wing of the police, it is also clear that it "will have the authority to strongly recommend that forces take action on any intelligence supplied" (Statewatch 1992 2(2): 10).

Importantly, NCIS will have its own computerized intelligence system, although at the time of writing its functional specification has not yet been agreed. The current project plan only allows national criminal intelligence staff to input information to the system. However, it is intended that police forces and regional crime squads will have terminals for inquiry purposes and that

Her Majesty's Customs and Excise will be allowed restricted access. The "Intelligence for input will come from UK forces, regional crime squads, Interpol, Her Majesty's Customs and Excise and other international law enforcement agencies" (*Hansard* 20 February 1992 cols 268-9).

The USA

For ease of exposition, the configuration of existing federal and state systems will be structured in terms of: the FBI systems, National Crime Information Center, the Identification Division and Triple I; followed by a brief description of some state systems. However, before detailing these systems, it is important to note their legal basis. Unlike the UK, the management of criminal history information is governed by overlapping federal, state, and local statutes, as well as executive orders. In that sense it is important to note that "existing computerized criminal history systems are inherently interorganizational systems with shared authority, control, and oversight" (Laudon 1986: 146).

The federal regulations are given in the 1975 Title 28, Code of Federal Regulations (USC) Part 20, Subparts B and C. State systems are given in Subpart B, and federal systems in Subpart C. In general, the effect of Title 28 has been to provide broad discretion to the FBI and the states to define standards for the interstate collection, maintenance, and disclosure of records. The Title 28 grants the FBI statutory authority to operate both the National Crime Information Center and the Identification Division, defining a range of authorized users of federal systems. The principal impact of Title 28 on federal systems has been to codify record contents, updating procedures, disclosures, and subject access (see US Department of Justice 1988 and chapter 5).

Title 28, Subpart B, regulates criminal history information in state and local systems funded in whole or in part by federal monies. This may be considered to include all state and local criminal justice agencies, non-criminal justice agencies, and individuals who use criminal history information in the USA. The most important result of Title 28 was the requirement that states establish a single, central repository either by statute or executive order. As with the FBI systems, Title 28 also requires specific standards on certain matters: completeness and accuracy; limitations on disclosure; record content; security; access and review; and audit. This last issue of audit requires states to record the names of all persons or agencies to whom information is disseminated, and the date on which it is disseminated. States are required to maintain a transaction log of who received what and to conduct audits of the procedures followed by local agencies to carry out state and federal laws.

Federal statute specifically provides for states to impose standards on their own state and local systems. Between 1974-1981, the LEAA monitored the progress on state legislation (see LEAA 1981). By the mid-1980s almost all states have established a central repository together with a regulatory authority. We now turn to the systems themselves.

National Crime Information Center

Managed and operated by the FBI, the National Crime Information Centre (NCIC) is a computer-based, national information system, the principal function of which is to support law enforcement and criminal justice activities, as well as non-criminal justice functions such as employment vetting. NCIC serves federal, state and local government agencies as well as private organizations (see Laudon 1986). It is located in the FBI's computer facility in Washington DC and includes a telecommunications network that reaches terminals in states. The telecommunications network allows for an estimated direct access by some 80 state and federal agencies, together with an estimated 64,000 other federal, state, and local law enforcement and criminal justice agencies entitled to access NCIC over these lines.

The NCIC consists of a number of data files, most of which furnish a bulletin board facility that is used by law enforcement agencies to list stolen/missing objects or wanted persons. In addition, there is a file, added in 1983 which contains a list of persons considered by the US Secret Service to be dangerous to the life of the President or other national figures. It is argued that this file allows tracking of these individuals. Until 1988, the NCIC also housed the Interstate Identification Index (see chapter 2) now renamed the Triple I. The Triple I is a sort of electronic directory or pointer to the criminal histories of over 12 million people in over twenty states. This Triple I system is now managed and maintained by the other federal system, the Identification Division (see below). At the end of 1988 (before Triple I was transferred to the Identification Division) the NCIC stored or indexed more than 20 million records. About 8 million on people or objects sought by law enforcement agencies (Gordon 1990: 44), with nearly one million transactions per day.

The criteria for including objects or persons in any of the NCIC files is a function both of the NCIC management policy and local discretion. Virtually any piece of stolen property which local agencies attest to being stolen can be included in the stolen property file, and any person for whom an arrest warrant has been issued can be included in the wanted persons file. NCIC maintains a list of around 1,200 offences classified as NCIC offences for which a person may be included in the system. This precludes minor misdemeanours, and some driving offences. However this varies by state.

On technology, until 1980 the FBI leased two IBM 360/65 computers , each with 2 million characters of memory. However, the age of the computers and peripheral devices created a situation by 1980 where maintaining the units was no longer cost effective. In 1982, two National Advanced Systems (NAS) AS/5000 computers, each with 4 million characters of memory replaced the old IBMs. New system requirements have been added since.

Laudon (1986) points out that NCIC operating costs have always been a matter of controversy, partly because costs are shared by the FBI and other users. The FBI pays for the central computer facilities and the communications links, while the users pay for the terminals and costs of gathering, inputting and processing the data at federal, state and local levels. The federal budget covers the cost to the FBI and to the federal agencies that use NCIC. State and local budgets cover most of the remaining costs.

NCIC interfaces with a number of criminal justice information systems operated by other federal, state and local agencies.

This includes the Identification Division, the National Law Enforcement Telecommunications System, the US Treasury Enforcement and Communication System, the Department of Justice Telecommunications System.

Under certain conditions, NCIC information is made available to other countries. Canada is the only country which can access NCIC data directly, with terminals under a reciprocal agreement. Other countries wishing to access the NCIC must do so through the US Drug Enforcement Administration which is the official liaison point with Interpol.

The Identification Division

This Division is essentially the fingerprint and criminal histories store. Prior to taking over the Triple I system, the file structure of the Identification Division was not as complex as the NCIC structure. The most significant event for the Division began in 1972 with the Automated Identification Division System (AIDS). In August 1973, AIDS-1 was implemented and resulted in the records of first offenders being placed on a computerized database. In 1979 the second phase occurred adding a name searching capability, and finally more recently the automated fingerprint searching capacity.

The AIDS system now contains over 10 million criminal history files and is growing at rate of 15,000 records per week (see Gordon 1990: 62). The development of the AIDS system overlapped the development of the Triple I system at NCIC since all records in the Triple I could have been found in either the automated or nonautomated files of the Identification Division. The FBI, was therefore, maintaining and operating two systems of criminal history records on individuals. For this reason, and as previously mentioned, the Triple I system was merged with Identification Division. Triple I functions as the development of the Interstate Identification Index concept (see chapter 2 for the background to the concept). There are two levels of participation in it. Full participation allows the state to add data as well as access data on file. If the state involved is not a full participant then data is on an access-only basis. All states are users of the system, but less than half are full and active participants.

The Identification Division differs from the NCIC in that all federal agencies have access. The Identification Division permits access to all state law enforcement agencies, and has been described as a central node in a network of federal and state systems.

State systems

The US Department of Justice could write in 1985 that in the last twenty years state central repositories of criminal history records "have been the focus of a data-gathering effort more massive and more coordinated than any other in criminal justice" (US Department of Justice 1985: 1). Forty-four states that responded to a 1985 survey reported holding some 35 million records (manual and automated) in their central repositories. Laudon (1986) suggests that at the local level the records probably rise to around 135 million. The ten most populous states have part or all of their central repository automated.

At the local level, most major metropolitan police departments use automated criminal justice information systems, and all have direct lines to the Identification Division and NCIC. On duty law enforcement officers can gain direct access to criminal history information in the state file through police patrol and inquiry systems. Automated systems and remote terminal access to state systems is now growing at an enormous rate.

In California, for example, the Criminal Justice Information System (CJIS) is located in the Bureau of Identification, Division of Law Enforcement of the Attorney General's Office. The CJIS is a multifile automated system, and has in excess of 5 million criminal histories. It is estimated that the number of transactions per year against files is in excess of 5 million. In New York, criminal information is divided between the Division of Criminal Justice Services and the New York State Police. Criminal history information, both manual and automated, is centralized in the Office of Identification in the Division of CJS. In 1986, there were 3.5 million records stored. The New York State Police operates the telecommunications network for the State of New York, which involves over 500 terminals connecting local agencies to state information files.

Figures from SEARCH Group and the US Department of Justice suggest that in excess of 50 per cent of all disclosures from the criminal history file are made at state level. Laudon (1986) makes the point that while relationships between state and federal systems are complex but capable of description, the relationship of the state central repositories to other state and local criminal justice and noncriminal justice systems virtually defies description.

Also at state level there exist intelligence information files. Gordon (1990) points out the characteristics of several of these systems. Most of these files are not on line but are accessible to law enforcement personnel via a telephone call. Often, as in New York, it is maintained by the state police. Some files that contain public information are organized in such a way as to be primarily useful for identifying suspects. Arizona law, for example, requires all those ever convicted of a sexual offence to register with the local sheriff when they move into an Arizona county (Arizona Criminal Code, art.13, sec 3821, 1988). This Sex Offender Registration Tracking Database is an on-line file that contains information provided by the registration and presumably serves as a suspect file when sexual offences occur.

According to Gordon (1990):

"Some states are hoping to automate investigative information on suspects for serious violent crimes and drug trafficking and put those records (or indexes to them) on-line, making them available – sometimes automatically, without a separate inquiry – to someone who calls up a warrant file or criminal history."   (Gordon ibid: 63).

Data quality, confidentiality and unauthorized disclosure

The UK

The issue of the accuracy and completeness of criminal records has been of concern for several years. Campbell & Connor (1986) quote instances of problems. For example:

"Ronald Powell, a black youth, spent a month in jail as a result of yet another mix-up. He was jailed after being arrested for affray, when magistrates were told of a long string of previous convictions including a six-month jail sentence. But the offences had been committed by a man called Newell; police had mixed up two similar criminal records numbers, and put Newell's offences into Powell's file at the Criminal Records Office." (Campbell & Connor ibid: 77).

While instances such as the one just described have been raised over the years, it has usually been in the context of discussions of abuses of individual civil liberties. It was not until 1990 that concerns about the national criminal record system as a whole became manifest.

Criticisms emerged during the House of Commons Home Affairs Committee's inquiry into the Crown Prosecution Service. During that inquiry the Committee received evidence from several witnesses that the criminal records provided to the courts and other agencies were inaccurate. The Law Society went further and described them as being "in a terrifying condition of inaccuracy" (House of Commons 1990a: para.1).

The Home Affairs Committee decided to make a separate inquiry into the state of the national criminal record system; their brief did not include a direct examination of intelligence held by the police nor the National Criminal Intelligence Service system which was then only at an early stage of discussion.

The Third Report of the House of Commons Home Affairs Committee for the Session 1989-90 provided an opportunity to focus on the state of criminal records for the first time in many years. Evidence was taken from the Home Office, The NIB, the Crown Prosecution Service, Justices' Clerks' Society, ACPO, the Data Protection Registrar and the Association of Chief Officers of Probation. The fragmentary nature of the criminal record system was noted, as was the slow method of keeping records up to date and there was little doubt "that the current arrangements are unsatisfactory" (House of Commons 1990a: para. 43).

Specifically, the Committee noted that evidence to it pointed to substantial increases in time taken by the police to inform NIB about charges, prosecutions, convictions and disposals. In 1980 it took 17 days, in 1989 it took an average of 27 days. Even more serious were the delays apparent in providing results of court proceedings to the NIB. As of 1 March, 1990, the average time for forces to notify results of cases was 77 days. Over 30,000 records were still incomplete after 30 months. On quality of the microfiche, there had been complaints about the legibility.

On disclosure the Home Affairs Committee was disturbed, given the sensitivity of criminal records, to find an essentially "ad hoc" set of arrangements. Within the criminal justice system, the Crown Prosecution Service gave evidence that records of convictions are submitted that are incorrect, incomplete, or out of date or contain extraneous and sometimes prejudicial material. Similarly, the Justices' Clerks' Society gave evidence relating to inaccuracy and incompleteness. On disclosure outside of the criminal justice system, the Home Affairs Committee was surprised at the current levels of Government vetting, and found such levels hard to justify. Disclosure to noncriminal justice agencies raised questions of to whom records are given, what information is available and the matter of correct matching of record to individual. The Committee concluded that on all three questions present arrangements do not provide satisfactory answers. In particular, it described the situation of discretionary disclosure by individual chief constables as having the potential to allow access in a haphazard and unaccountable manner with worrying implications for the liberty of the individual.

The Home Affairs Committee was aware that computerization was the long term goal for criminal records but before that it recommended that the Home Office and Lord Chancellor's Department should lay down specified times for getting information in to the system. The delay of an average 77 days to input a court decision was blamed on officers having no 'ownership' of the problem, but was none the less unsatisfactory for all that. As and when computerization took place, the Committee wanted to see inputs made by court clerks rather than police officers, as a way of improving the time rate, and for the criminal record at national level to be expanded to include all recordable offences; it was recommended that transfer to the PNC be completed by the end of 1994. In achieving the transfer it was hoped that a system could be found for separating out factual material such as the record of convictions from prejudicial material such as intelligence data.

On other matters, the Home Affairs Committee suggested that on disclosure, applicants should always receive a copy of their record to check it. Overall vetting was to be handed from the police to a new independent agency (a National Criminal Records Authority). This Authority, as well as maintaining the system would also agree information policies – for example the criteria for disclosure to other bodies.

Technological advances in the field of automatic fingerprint recognition and DNA profiles (genetic fingerprinting) were recommended to improve accuracy and the scope for identification. Although the NIB held the national fingerprint collection for England and Wales, it had no equivalent automatic recognition system of the kind in Scotland. A 1988 Audit Report had been very critical of the organization of fingerprint filing systems (Audit Commission 1988). DNA fingerprinting seemed to offer an additional sophisticated and accurate form of identification by analyzing personal samples. Genetic material from the scene of a crime could be matched against a databank of DNA profiles (digitally stored). Indeed, the Committee added its voice to the growing calls for a national DNA database to be "closely co-ordinated with the computerization of the National Collection of Criminal Records " (House of Commons 1990a: para. 27).

The Government responded to these criticisms and recommendations in July 1990 (Home Office 1990a). The overall solution to the problem, as far as the

Government was concerned, lay in computerization. However, a number of short term measures were also outlined. On specific recommendations, the Government felt it necessary to leave the activities of court officials and police who input records to the NIB, to local management in the light of local circumstances. Following full computerization, it was agreed that inputs should be made by court clerks, but that a demand to expand the record content needed to be weighed against the resource implications that would be involved. The extracting of prejudicial material from NIB records was to be carried out by the police and force NIB liaison officers given advice on how this should operate.

The Government was not persuaded that there was need to establish a statutory independent agency to maintain and process criminal records, and it agreed to look again at how vetting arrangements might be improved. A commitment was made to introduce Automatic Fingerprint Recognition and the need for a DNA database was accepted and was already the subject of discussion between the NIB and the Forensic Science Service. Elsewhere such DNA developments were viewed more critically in terms of security, relevance and retention (Cohen 1991) and also the admissibility of DNA evidence to courts (see for example McLeod 1991). Of more general importance was the Governments intention to commission an 'efficiency scrutiny' of the whole criminal records system to be carried out by the Home Office. The results of the scrutiny were reported in late 1991 (Home Office 1991) and are considered in chapter 7.

In June 1991, prior to the publication of the Home Office Scrutiny Report, the National Council for Civil Liberties delivered its own report on the current criminal record and information system (NCCL 1991). The NCCL report considered the way in which information is collected, the scope and nature of the records and finally disclosure matters.

NCCL agreed with the concerns of the Home Affairs Committee about the accuracy of conviction data, but NCCL was much more concerned about the "unacceptable ways in which other information – the criminal and political intelligence information – is collected, held and used" (NCCL ibid: 3), and it is this type of information that the report deals with. It is critical of the use of police stop and search powers to augment information databases. In addition, it raises concerns about the maintenance on computer of the information resulting from large-scale inquiries – where large numbers of people are questioned and data being essentially a mixture of fact and speculation. NCCL cite several instances of complaint on this issue. In relation to the gathering of information, the 1984 Data Protection Act effectively exempts the police from abiding by the First Data Protection Principle, which requires data users to obtain and process information fairly and lawfully; the NCCL correctly point out that the Data Protection Registrar has no powers to enforce this Principle where to do so would be likely to prejudice the prevention or detection of crime. On a related point, NCCL also point out that the police may obtain information from sources who have not registered their intention to disclose information to the police. Under section 28(3) of the Act, any data user may disclose information to the police when the disclosure is for the purpose of the prevention and detection of crime or the apprehension or prosecution of offenders. NCCL cite some disturbing instances of these matters.

In relation to the scope and nature of criminal records, the NCCL report states that the:

> "criminal information system must be viewed as a whole. Increasing computerization – and, particularly the linkage of computers – means that all this information may be integrated into a large national information system. To consider the question of criminal records in isolation would be a merely superficial exercise ducking the more controversial aspects of the information held by the police." (NCCL ibid: 7)

There is concern about the particularly worrisome state of local records, and the NCCL agree with the Home Affairs Committee that the Association of Chief Police Officers (ACPO) should issue guidance to all forces to achieve consistency of approach and content.

In relation to the operation and structure of the PNC2, NCCL is concerned about the linking of the criminal names index with the wanted/missing persons index which, according to NCCL, contained criminal intelligence data. Similarly, on warning signals on the PNC2, NCCL raise the issue of whether such descriptions, including that fact of a person's HIV/AIDS status, is justified.

The report is highly critical of the 1984 Data Protection Act and what NCCL sees as the Act's inability to connect with the realities of police information exchange. The files held under criminal intelligence categories are, in practice, exempt from the 'subject access' disclosure under the Act. The police are entitled to withhold disclosure when to do so is likely to prejudice the 'prevention or detection of crime' or the 'apprehension or prosecution of offenders'.

The NCCL report also points out that while the 1984 Data Protection Act has its origins in the Council of Europe Convention on Data Processing, the UK Government has entered reservations to certain parts of the sector specific use of police data (Council of Europe, Recommendation (87)15).

The reservations cover collection of data and mean that unlike the other 24 members of the Council of Europe, the UK police have no obligation to inform individuals about data having been collected on them, and the UK police are also free to collect so called sensitive data on people solely on the basis that they have a particular racial origin, sexual behaviour or political opinions.

Finally on authorized disclosure, the NCCL report shares the concerns raised by the Home Affairs Committee, and cites several disturbing employment case studies, arguing for more effective safeguards (NCCL 1991: 16-18).

As previously indicated, in principle where no statutory requirement exists, the decision whether or not to disclose information in police records rests with the chief constable, although there is Home Office guidance which provides a general principle of confidentiality. However, over the years there has been continuing disquiet about the extent of unauthorized disclosure by police officers to others. This misuse has been explored by several authors over the years (see Rule 1973; Bunyan 1976; Draper 1978; Campbell & Connor 1986). Bunyan (1976) describes several examples of informal, unauthorized disclosure from the 1970s which used private tracing agencies. These agencies employed ex-policemen used to making requests to criminal record offices, and who - given the demands on CROs telephones - experienced little difficulty because it was impossible to verify each call. Again, the picture in the late 1960s and early 1970s is one where, according to James Rule the misuse of information was commonplace:

"The vulnerability of these offices (CROs) is especially great to former members of the police, who are invariably well versed in the techniques of making such requests. Industrial firms employ retired policemen in large numbers as security officers, precisely because of their familiarity with police routines in these and other matters. In many cases too, the personal ties between these private security officers and former colleagues make it possible for them to obtain services which would be denied to others."

(Rule ibid: 82)

In a similar vein, Prince (1982) writing in *Police Review*, note: "Police officers in the United Kingdom have always been involved in the vetting of employees in the private sector...". He continues, "These checks were usually made under 'the Old Pals Act', and if any reward were received by the police officer it was nothing more than the occasional liquid refreshment." (Prince ibid: 737). However, he then points out in the same 1982 article that such illegal checks made on employees and prospective employees are running at a low level compared with the past. This view of the demise of or at least diminution in misuse is echoed elsewhere, and is based on the view that police officers had learned from the experience of the 1974 Rehabilitation of Offenders Act, which made it a criminal offence for an officer to disclose 'other than in the course of official duties'. However, this is unlikely given the very low level of prosecutions under this provision, and the arcane complexities of bringing an action under this part of the 1974 Act (see Breed nd: 69-74). Breed cites several cases including the following:

"A man was convicted of theft in 1973 and sentenced to a fine of £ 50. It was his first and only conviction. Under the terms of the Rehabilitation of Offenders Act the conviction became spent by 1979. Yet in 1984 information about this minor conviction was revealed by the police to a prospective employer, and the offer of the job was withdrawn. There is even one case of a man who was acquitted of an offence but who still apparently has 'a record' which the police are able to reveal. In fact, this is a case of an 'unauthorized disclosure' of an 'unauthorized record'. He was acquitted in 1981 of theft from his employers in circumstances which made it obvious that he had been framed by those same employers. He even succeeded in a claim for unfair dismissal...After being unemployed for some time he was offered a job, but was dismayed when the offer was withdrawn. The firm that had made the job offer told him the reason was that he had a police record, and actually admitted that their information had been obtained from the police."   (Breed ibid: 71)

More recent evidence suggest that any sanguine view that these are activities of the past is misplaced. For example, the Apex Trust, a Home Office funded organization concerned with employment policies for ex-offenders, gave evidence to the House of Commons Employment Committee on the matter of unauthorized disclosure. On the basis of a national survey of employers, "56 per cent took steps to 'confirm' the records of job applicants. Although not all of these were claiming indirect access to police records, a significant number of companies certainly were." (Minutes of Evidence, *Recruitment Practices*, Session 1989-90, HC 409- ii: 21).

In addition, Whitcher and Jones (1989) in their survey of Volunteer Bureaux found that in excess of 50 per cent of replies were positive to the question "Are informal methods of police checking (i.e. outside the officially authorized categories) carried out in your area?". The recent Home Office Scrutiny Report (Home Office 1991: para. 155) gives details of unauthorized disclosure of criminal intelligence to 'trusted' colleagues in local authority social services departments. In a similar vein, the 1990 Annual Report of the Police Complaints Authority expresses concern that there has been "a noticeable increase in the number of complaints about police officers making use of the police national computer or force intelligence records for other than official purposes." (Annual Report of the Police Complaints Authority ibid: para 2.6). Finally, cases appearing in national newspapers continue unabated:

- Winchester Crown Court case (*Independent* 3.2.89)
- disclosure of record in Wiltshire to employer (*Independent* 15.2.90)
- Stevens Inquiry in N. Ireland on police links with Ulster Defence Association (*Independent*, 18.5.90 and 11.10.90)
- vetting of security staff for Polly Peck (*Observer* 29.9.91)
- 'Guardian Angels' connection with Metropolitan police vetting (*Manchester Evening News* 23.11.91).

The USA

Data quality issues, confidentiality and unauthorized disclosure have been issues of major importance and concern in the USA, and the approach to data quality in particular has been much more structured than in the UK. This is not only because this is a matter of importance in itself, but also because of the growing recognition of the extensive use of criminal records within and without the criminal justice system. In what follows, we attempt to briefly summarize the main issues and concerns.

The Privacy Act of 1974, which establishes standards for personal records maintained by federal agencies and some federal contractors, excluded specific provision for law enforcement files until such time as more comprehensive criminal justice legislation was passed. However as Gordon (1990) notes that time never came. Although hearings were held on half a dozen criminal justice bills, none ever passed. Nevertheless, spurred on by the 1975 SEARCH Group document *Technical Report No 13: Standards for the Security and Privacy of Criminal History Record Information*, the LEAA issued federal regulations in 1976 requiring state and local systems receiving federal funding to establish procedures to ensure the accuracy and completeness of records. As Laudon (1986) points out, while there was recognition of the growing importance of data quality in criminal record systems, methodologies for examining record quality were not established and there were few empirical studies. In response, Laudon and colleagues undertook a research study from 1979-1982 using three methods: surveys of end users or clients; samples of entire record files; samples of active or current cases. They examined files at the NCIC, the Identification Division and state files. What did they find?

In relation to the Identification Division files, just over 25 per cent were complete, accurate, and unambiguous, whereas nearly 75 per cent exhibited some significant quality problems. Translated to the number of 2.35 million annual record disclosures, Laudon points out that the results indicate that 1.75 million of the disclosures had a significant quality problem. The most common problem was lack of court disposition information, followed by inaccurate recording and ambiguity of record.

The analysis of the NCIC files found 45 per cent of records were complete, accurate and unambiguous, with 55 per cent having some significant quality problem. Here, as in the primarily manual Identification Division, the most frequent problem involved lack of disposition data, with the next most serious problem involving inaccuracy of disposition recording.

The findings of Laudon's study for state files were similar to those at federal level. In three state systems, the level of data quality ranged from only 12.2 per cent of recently disclosed records being accurate, complete and unambiguous in one state, to 18.9 per cent in a second state, and 49.4 in the final state. In all states, the most significant problem involved lack of disposition information, followed by incomplete records, inaccuracy of recorded dispositions, and ambiguity of information. Laudon concludes "While there is a considerable range in data quality among the states, it would appear fair to conclude that data quality problems in state systems are far greater than is commonly known and more significant than previously imagined." (Laudon ibid: 143).

Although inadequate disposition reporting is by far the most common and serious quality problem found in criminal history records, there are other problems as well. In a national survey, criminal justice officials estimated that between 20 and 35 per cent of records in most systems are materially inaccurate or ambiguous (SEARCH Group 1985).

However it is not surprising that there is a problem at the state level. A US Department of Justice report in 1988 revealed that while all state central record repositories require arrest data, fewer than half expressly require the reporting of court dispositions. Only thirteen states require the central repository to conduct an annual audit of state and local records submitted to the system, and only eleven require the repository to audit its own records annually (US Department of Justice 1988: 4-5). The meaning of a particular record is unclear unless it indicates that the arrest ended in an acquittal, dismissal, conviction, or was simply not prosecuted. This is especially important since almost all evidence points to the fact that few arrests result in conviction. A 1988 report of the Bureau of Justice Statistics looked at data from nine states concerning arrest for serious crimes and found a variation from 50 per cent resulting in conviction in Ohio to 79 per cent in Utah. In 1984 in eleven states only 55 per cent of felony arrest for violent offences, 66 per cent for property offences, and

54 per cent for drug offences led to conviction (US Department of Justice, Bureau of Justice Statistics *Bulletin* January 1988).

It is difficult to not to agree with commentators who interpret the available research findings as indicating that:

a.   constitutional rights of due process are not well protected in either manual or computerized criminal history systems;

b.   the efficiency and effectiveness of law enforcement or criminal justice programmes which rely on such records must be impaired considerably. Maintenance of due process standards cannot be assured in administrative processes reliant upon fundamentally incomplete, inaccurate and ambiguous information. Disclosure of incomplete records which indicate stigmatizing arrests but not exonerating dispositions not only overstate the proven criminality of individuals but deny employment to persons with little justification in law.

While the research paints a bleak picture, it is important to recognize that the 1975 SEARCH Group standards have had an impact, although perhaps limited. In that context the revised 1988 standards (SEARCH Group 1988) hold mixed grounds for optimism. While the technical standards are detailed, the principles on which they are based are clear:

- that the states should have exclusive control over criminal history information that they create or receive, except for such limitations as may be necessary in order to participate effectively in interstate programmes of exchange

- that noncriminal justice agencies may have a legitimate need for access to criminal history information

- that in so far as is possible, all criminal history data should be disclosed only on the basis of positive identification by means of fingerprints

- that state and local agencies should implement safeguards in order to enhance the security of manual and automated criminal justice information systems

- that agencies should implement certain enumerated programmes that have proven to be effective in improving the accuracy, completeness and timeliness of criminal justice information

- that agencies should establish programmes for auditing criminal history information systems.

In this context, it is also clear that the related issue of concerns on confidentiality has influenced the adoption of revised standards. Of primary concern, is the continued erosion of statutory confidentiality protection for criminal history information. Since 1979, several states, including, most notably, Florida and Oklahoma, have adopted open record statutes under which the public can obtain virtually all criminal record information. In addition, in recent years, legislatures in many states have adopted legislation which authorizes or requires state repositories and/or other criminal justice agencies to make criminal history information available to particular types of noncriminal justice requesters for particular purposes. Most common are statutes permitting or requiring the release of information for background checks on those who work with children or in other sensitive positions. The Congress has made piecemeal exceptions to comprehensive confidentiality safeguards with respect to criminal records. Today, federal-held records can be released for background employment checks at certain banking institutions and securities organizations. In 1985, moreover, Congress enacted the Security Clearance Information Act, which requires state and local record release for national security checks. In 1986, Congress enacted the Immigration Reform Act, which again allows disclosure about illegal aliens who are applying for eligibility for citizenship under the Act's programme. All these issues of authorized disclosure are more fully discussed in chapter 5.

However, it is important to conclude this chapter by noting that on the matter of misuse of records or unauthorized disclosure there are similar parallels with the experience of the UK. Laudon (1986) in the course of his research documents several instances of police and other officials who exchanged criminal record information with credit companies and large department stores, and several instances of internal subversion of data processing clerks, resulting in large-scale diversions of criminal records to outside interests. Sometimes the prevention of crime becomes the justification for an illegal use. In Louisiana, for example, despite state legislation calling for the privacy and security of information contained in the central repository, it became common practice in New Orleans for employers needing an unauthorized record check to obtain it through personal contacts with people in the law enforcement agency. Finally, several commentators have discovered instances in which police undercover units create false criminal history records in order to provide cover for police agents engaged in undercover police work. One police chief reported:

> "If these criminal history systems were ships, they would never be able to float because of all the leaks. We're essentially forced to create phoney records in order to cover our people because we know that members of organized crime have access to these systems." (Laudon ibid: 94)

4 Criminal records – Uses within the criminal justice system

Introduction

The main objective in storing criminal records has always been to assist the smooth running of the criminal justice system. This was the historical reason for bringing records into existence and remains the priority reason for their accumulation. In recent years, as we shall explore in subsequent chapters, disclosures outside of the criminal justice system have grown considerably, but first let us consider the use of criminal records within that system.

A criminal justice system is a disparate entity consisting of different personnel and practitioners playing different roles and representing different individual and organisational interests. The main actors include the police, judiciary, lawyers, social workers and probation officers who collectively 'process' a person from suspect through to arrestee, defendant and finally an acquittal or conviction and sentenced person. The process is overseen by the public as represented by the press and the sentenced person is taken from the justice system by representatives of the penal system including officers of the prison service. The process can be viewed as a series of decisions being made by the practitioners concerned with their various ideologies and objectives and differing forms of accountability. Responsibility for the system ultimately rests with those with political oversight and it is given direction by senior judicial officers.

Within the criminal justice system criminal records are required for 'investigative purposes' by the police and other criminal detection agencies, and for 'judicial purposes' by other agencies of the system. The two 'purposes' are not entirely separate and there is a degree of overlap, for example, where police are empowered to 'caution' people who admit their guilt in certain circumstances, or prosecution agencies use records to determine whether or not to pursue a prosecution. Within these terms the use of criminal records within the criminal justice system can be represented in diagram form (figure 7). The intention here will be to explore the different uses made of criminal records by the various parts of the system in England and Wales and to compare and contrast that use with other criminal justice systems as appropriate.

Figure 7
Disclosure of criminal records within the criminal justice system

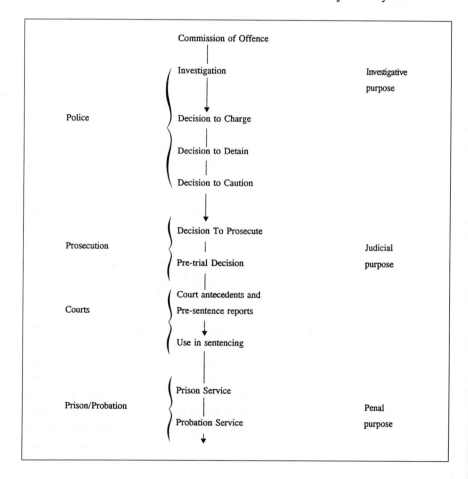

The investigative purpose

The police would contend that the maintenance of criminal record systems is primarily to assist them in their policing activities and it is in particular the prevention of crime and detection of criminals on which we will concentrate in this chapter. In carrying out this investigative function a representative of the International Association of Chiefs of Police has emphasised that "timely information is the lifeblood of a police agency" and for that reason law enforcement agencies are "eager to play a major role in assuring that high quality criminal history records information is available" (Summers 1986: 28).

It has been suggested that detectives have two broad responsibilities, which are firstly the collection of information on crimes committed and secondly the collection of information that will ultimately lead to evidence for a prosecution (Carling and Burrows 1985). Our purpose here, is to examine that secund function and to see how criminal records are part of a wider scan of information used by the police in the investigation of crime.

Examined in this way the investigation of crime is effectively a search for information that will help police officers to make a decision on a suspect, arrestee and the person they would wish to see prosecuted before the courts. It is the skill of the detective to carry out this search and to use all available sources to assist identification of the alleged offender. In so doing reference will be made to information already stored by the police and including criminal history records, other intelligence held by the police, information from scenes of crime and from the victims and witnesses of crime and also information obtained from the questioning of suspects.

In England and Wales the police are given powers by the Police and Criminal Evidence Act 1984 to stop and search individuals for information and to enter premises in the pursuit of an investigation. Orders can also be obtained through a circuit judge to order the production of other information to the police investigating serious crime whether this is held by individuals or organisations. Procedural arrangements are in place to assist the input of information from local authority agencies to the police (see eg. Hebenton and Thomas 1992) and from national agencies such as social security offices (see Home Office 1986 (c): para 1.79).

Law enforcement agencies also keep their own records to assist investigations, including criminal photographs and fingerprints, details of vehicle registrations and data banks of 'intelligence'. As we have seen (chapter 3) these repositories of information, increasingly held on computers, may be categorised as 'hard' verifiable information such as a conviction record, and the 'soft' more speculative information designated as intelligence and including, for example, people who might become offenders. We have also seen how these repositories may be held regionally for local police forces, centrally for national forces and how current developments are in the direction of international data banks of personal information for police use. (for an account of the development of UK police use of computers see Newing 1990)

We have identified the UK's Police National Computer and the categories of information held which are available to all police stations within seconds throughout the UK and including the Isle of Man and the Channel Islands. We have also referred to the National Identification Bureau on the third floor at New Scotland Yard and the Criminal Record Office of the police forces in Scotland, held in Glasgow. The Royal Ulster Constabulary have access to the mainland PNC through the Merseyside police, but also hold their own criminal record collection.

British police forces keep some criminal records of their own as well as intelligence records at a local level in 'collators' offices where they can almost constitute a street by street analysis, in some areas. Mostly these have been manual files with only some attempts to place the information on computer such as Greater Manchester Police's MANCRO system. At a national level we have witnessed the evolution of the idea of a national computerised data base for criminal intelligence on serious crimes and its manifestation 1st April 1992 as the National Criminal Intelligence System (NCIS). NCIS will start operations using PNC facilities, but by 1995 will have its own computer systems.

In the USA we have also noted the importance of the National Crime Information Centre (NCIC) and its service operated by the FBI to all state police forces. The NCIC holds 19 million records on fugitives, stolen vehicles and criminal histories. The FBI also has its Identification Search and has been instrumental in starting the Interstate Identification Index, both available to state forces who, in addition, also have their own data bases.

Canada has developed its Canadian Police Information Centre (CPIC) since 1972 to service the whole country from its base in Ottawa. At a national level CPIC is used by the Royal Canadian Mounted Police and at a local level by provincial and urban forces. Of particular note are the Criminal Record Synopsis File and the Personal file on people wanted by the police. Running alongside CPIC is the Criminal Intelligence Service Canada with its national Automated Criminal Intelligence Information System. At a local level most provincial forces have their own information systems and the Ontario Provincial Police have their own computerised intelligence service. At an international level CPIC has an inter-face with the US National Crime Information Centre. (Flaherty 1986 (b)).

European police forces have their own repositories of criminal records, and the European police have also been active in developing close cooperation and international data base arrangements for the trans-border flow of personal information; these systems are referred to in Chapter 7. The most comprehensive system of international police information exchange is through the International Criminal Police Organisation better known as Interpol. From its computerised headquarters in Lyon, it can assist police investigations on a world-wide basis (see also Chapter 7). Within Europe the UK police have been assisted by the UK's adoption of the European Convention on Mutual Assistance in Criminal Matters in 1991 (Foreign and Commonwealth Affairs Office 1991: see esp. Articles 13 and 22) and the passing of the 1990 Criminal Justice (International Cooperation) Act.

With access to all of these sources of police held information the task of the investigating officer is still to identify a person who may have committed the particular recorded crime under investigation. Local routine inquiries will not always necessarily require the full national and international resources available.

Other technical aids to assist the investigating officer include computer free Text Retrieval facilities that will scan names, lists of vehicles and so on for matches based on particular information. Similarly for fingerprint matching, systems of Automatic Fingerprint Recognition (AFR) or the American Automated Fingerprint Identification Systems (AFIS) have been developed to assist rapid identification. Photographs of known offenders can be more swiftly examined through video display units using optical discs knows as Product Retrieval on Optical Disc (PROD), and systems are being developed for computer matching of faces recorded on security cameras on the WIZARD system (see NCCL 1991).

Future developments for the UK include the possible introduction of identity cards to compensate for the reduction in border controls in a frontier-free Europe (see NCCL 1988) and the use of DNA blood testing to assist identification and the spectre of future data banks containing the DNA genetic 'fingerprints' of the whole population. The Data Protection Registrar in the UK, has reported his belief that, "whereas until now talk of establishing large scale (DNA) databases has been premature for a number of purely practical reasons, such a prospect may soon become a realistic possibility" (DPR 1992: 8).

Already developed and in use in the UK is the computer assisted search and analysis of information for investigating officers carried out by the Home Office Large Major Enquiry Systems (HOLMES). HOLMES is the outcome of work that followed a critical report from H.M. Inspectors of Constabulary into the conduct of the, "Yorkshire Ripper" inquiries by the West Yorkshire police, and has been operational since 1985. At the time of writing, "the development of HOLMES Mark II is high on the list of national IT requirements". (Newing 1990 ; see also Ackroyd *et al* 1992: 150-156)

All of these technological developments are intent on improving police efficiency and effectiveness in the detection and prosecution of criminals. In processing personal information on people, the developments are all subject, to a greater or lesser extent, to forms of regulation in the interests of privacy and data protection. The interests of police investigations and the protection of privacy through data protection regulations are inevitably going to be in conflict. As Flaherty has identified the tension:

"There are clear limits to the power of a data protection authority. If a government is determined to introduce a practice that may be, at least in part, highly invasive of personal privacy".   (Flaherty 1986 (a))

In the UK the 1984 Data Protection Act has sought to regulate the computer use of all forms of personal information, including that held by the police. The Act, however, offers exemptions to some of its provisions to police forces using information to detect crime (S.28). In general terms much of the Act does still apply to police use of personal information, including their need to register as 'users' with the Data Protection Registrar and allow 'subjects' access to information held on them. The Association of Chief Police Officers (ACPO) has produced its own voluntary Code of Practice based on provisions of the Act (ACPO 1987).

The Council of Europe has given advice to its member states concerning the regulation of personal information used by the police. Its Recommendation R (84) 10 started a debate on standards of quality and disclosure of criminal record information (Council of Europe 1984) that was followed up by the wider ranging Recommendation R (87) 15 (Council of Europe 1988). The latter Recommendation requires police authorities, for example, not to collect information on individuals without notifying them, unless it would prejudice an inquiry, and not to collect data on people simply on the basis of racial origin, religious convictions, sexual behaviour or political opinions. The UK Government has reserved its right to not comply with either of these two particular requirements (see Hansard 15.10.90 cols 721-2).

In the USA the Privacy Act 1974 has proved to be a relatively ineffective form of data protection compared to European state laws (see Flaherty 1986 (b)). With no equivalent office of Data Protection Commissioner or Registrar the regulation of police held information, including criminal records came from the Law Enforcement Assistance Administration (LEAA) which is now part of the Department of Justice. The LEAA produced its 1976 Regulations which influenced the quality and accessibility of criminal records in every State. At the same time the State funded SEARCH organisation, the National Consortium for Justice Information and Statistics, produced its Technical Report No.13 into Standards for the Security and Privacy of Criminal History Record Information, giving non-statutory advice to all States on the maintenance and use of criminal records in all respects including investigative purposes. The Report has been subsequently updated (SEARCH 1988).

One question raised in a number of countries concerns the status of police information, to the effect that an investigation of a particular person is actually going on or that a person has been arrested by the police. In the USA it has been held that information concerning arrests is in the public domain following the 1976 case of Paul v Davis in Kentucky (see US Dept. of Justice 1988: 14 ff), whilst in the UK it has been held that the press have no automatic right to know from the police the name of a person being investigated or who has been charged with a criminal offence (Rv. Sec. of State for the Home Department ex p. Westminster Press Law Report *The Independent* 21.1.92).

The UK ruling appears to contradict an earlier ruling that a newspaper publishing a mans previous convictions during a police hunt for him was not necessarily in common law contempt of court even thought the police had requested that no publicity be given to the convictions. It was held that the editor had no intent to prejudice the administration of justice by way of any future proceedings by publishing the information and accepted his view of the 'public interest' in publishing (Attorney General v Sports Newspapers Law Report, The Guardian 19.6.91).

Police discretion is also permitted, to enable disclosure of a relevant arrest to an employer. The Home Office has given guidance to the British police on circumstances when this should take place (Home Office 1986 (a) Schedule 2) and is aimed at situations where the arrest and alleged offence might interfere with the persons ability to continue working. Evidence has also come to light of some police forces developing particular policies of employer notification on arguably less relevant offences such as 'kerb-crawling' but where the embarrassment effect might be an effective deterrent (see *The Independent* 13.11.89).

Other police decisions

Although investigation and detection may be the prime use to which the police put criminal records, there are also allied decisions which they have to make and criminal records can also inform these decisions. These include the need to continue a police detention, decisions regarding alternatives to prosecution and decisions concerning the need for an immediate charge and court appearance or a more considered decision to report a case with a view to a later summons.

Police detention may be needed for additional time to question a suspect and for holding a charged suspect before a court appearance. The existence of previous conviction information will need to be balanced with existing inquiries and the nature of the offence being investigated. Extended detention without charge would be a decision for a senior officer or magistrate. Following a charge a senior officer would rule on the detention before court.

In England and Wales juveniles who the police feel should be detained prior to going to court, would normally be passed to the care of the local authority to be looked after in a childrens' home. The police can hold the juveniles in a police station rather than pass them over, if they consider local authority care 'impractical' or inappropriate in the case of a juvenile aged over 15 charged with an offence involving violence or sexual connotations. Criminal history records would be assessed in making such decisions (Police and Criminal Evidence Act 1984 s.38 as amended by Criminal Justice Act 1991).

Policies of 'diversion' are intended to keep certain offenders out of the criminal justice system altogether. Police officers can use their discretion to discontinue arrangements for prosecution in favour of the lesser disposal of 'cautioning' an offender. The practice is aimed primarily at juvenile offenders, but also at people with mental health problems, elderly people and people known to be habitually drunken offenders. A person can only be cautioned in the UK if there has been an admission of guilt made to the police.

The Home Office has encouraged the development of liaison panels between police officers and other professionals such as social workers and probation officers to assist in the making of a decision to caution. These juvenile liaison panels or juvenile bureaux will meet at periodic intervals to consider named juveniles who have admitted their guilt. In determining the need for a court hearing various social factors will be taken into account as well as the existence of a criminal record. Diversion from courts is premised on the belief that court hearings can lead to 'labelling' of offenders and play a part in amplifying their deviance (see eg. Thorpe et al 1980).

The Home Office suggests that within these deliberations the existence of previous convictions "is an important factor, although not in itself decisive":

"a previous conviction or caution should not rule out a subsequent caution if other factors suggest it might be suitable".

(Home Office 1990 (b): Annex B para 3)

Research into the use of cautions for both juveniles and adults revealed their use overwhelmingly on first time offenders with only a small number of offenders receiving more than two cautions, (Evans and Wilkinson 1990).

Although cautions are to achieve a disposal outside of the criminal justice system their existence is recorded within it. The Home Office has recommended that they be included in the proposed national criminal record collection to avoid them being overlooked in smaller local repositories (Home Office 1991: para 83). Cautions will be included in antecedent reports made to courts (see also Home Office 1978). This contradiction between devices designed to keep people out of the criminal justice system still resulting in records being accumulated inside the system is part of the widely recognised phenomena of net-widening (see Cohen 1985: 52).

The court

The forum of the public court hearing represents a symbolic central point in the criminal justice system. Police information and intelligence may be received by the court as evidence of the particular charge under scrutiny, whilst at the end of the hearing following a finding of guilt and a conviction, previous criminal conviction records will be made available as antecedents to assist the courts sentence and disposal decisions.

In England and Wales attempts have been made to improve the flow of all criminal information and other relevant data between the constituent parts of the criminal justice system. In 1989 a Steering Committee was established with representatives from all the courts, the police, probation service, the prison service and the Crown Prosecution Service, with, "its principle aim ... to improve the efficiency of data interchange, exploiting where appropriate the benefits of information technology" (Waugh 1991: 28). The Steering Committee in turn developed into the initiative known as the Coordination of Computerisation in the Criminal Justice System (CCCJS).

Working groups have been established to look at Standard Specifications for Computerisation in the Crown Prosecution Service (SCOPE), the Crown Court (CREST) and the Magistrates Courts (MASS). (see figure 8)

In the magistrates courts, for example, information technology would assist with scheduling of cases, tracking of fine defaulters and the issuing of warrants and would link the magistrates courts directly to the Probation Service, the National Criminal Records System, Police Administration Support Units and the Crown Prosecution Service (Home Office 1990 (c)). The Working Groups report to the Committee for the Coordination of Computerisation in the

Criminal Justice System (see also Pape, 1992; Lord Chancellors Department 1992: chapter 11).

Figure 8
Proposed computerisation of UK Criminal Justice System

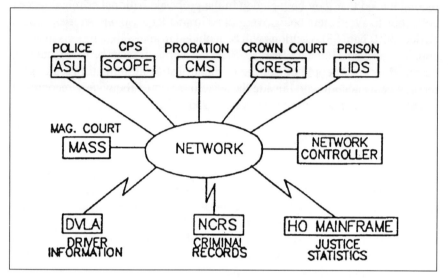

Abbreviations:

ASH	-	Administrative Support Unit
DVLA	-	Driver and Vehicle Licensing
SCOPE	-	Crown Prosecution Service
NCRS	-	National Criminal Records System
CMS-HO	-	Probation Service
CREST	-	Ccown Court Electronic Support
LIDS	-	Local Inmates Database System
MASS	-	Magistrates Courts Standard System

We should also note that personnel within a court may find themselves the subject of criminal record disclosures. Magistrates have their criminal record history investigated at the point of application to become a magistrate and are also liable to be reported in the event that they commit an offence during their term as a magistrate. Judges, barristers and solicitors may also be reported to their professional bodies or the Lord Chancellor's Department if they are found to commit an offence whilst practising or holding office. Probation officers, social workers and the police are all vetted at the point of admission to their professions (see chapters 5 and 6; Home Office 1986 (b)).

The vetting of jurors by reference to police records is a practice that has existed for some years and gives power to prosecutors to have a juror 'stood by' if considered unsuitable. Until the mid-1970's "no one appears to have displayed much public interest in the precise source of the prosecutors information" (Leigh 1980: 159). After some Parliamentary probing the Attorney General published the Code of Practice covering jury vetting in *The Times* (11 Oct 1978). Today the law has been clarified in the Juries (Disqualification) Act 1984 with the Code of Practice guiding in depth vetting of jurors in cases of terrorism or national security with random criminal record checking being carried out on jurors in other cases (see Home Office 1988a).

Pre-trial court proceedings

Before a trial is ready to proceed a court may be called on to make other decisions. Principal amongst these are the decision to adjourn and remand a defendant on bail or in custody, and decisions made in committal proceedings to bring a defendant before a different court. There is no requirement to consider criminal records in making these decisions.

In England and Wales a magistrate court may commit a defendant for trial in the more senior Crown Court if it thinks the offence is particularly serious and may require powers of punishment greater than those available to the magistrates court. In making this decision the magistrate can consider other information available to it, but not information concerning previous convictions (Rv. Colchester Justices ex parte North Essex Building Co. Ltd. 1977 3 All ER 567).

A magistrates court having convicted a defendant has the power to commit the defendant to a Crown Court to receive a higher sentence. Having accepted jurisdiction for the case at the beginning this can only be done if 'new evidence' has come to light during proceedings. 'New evidence' might include antecedents revealing a history of previous convictions (Magistrates Courts Act 1980 s38) or after offences revealed by the defendant that he wants taking into consideration.

Conviction and sentencing: procedures and practice

Following a court hearing of evidence for the prosecution and for the defence, two decisions are made: conviction and sentence. The former is the finding of guilt or innocence, the latter the form of disposal considered necessary following a conviction.

Throughout a court hearing and up until the point of conviction, procedure in the UK, and many other countries will not permit the disclosure of criminal records in court. Previous convictions will be revealed in the antecedents report made available after conviction and prior to sentence. This so called 'shield of protection' is to uphold the principle that a defendant should only be tried for the offence with which he is charged and not for offences he has already been tried for.

Critics of the procedure to withhold convictions during a trial regard it as an outdated procedure. A spokesman for the police has asked:

"Why can't his previous record, if relevant to that case be known to a jury? How many times have we seen a jury shocked and distressed to discover the real history of a criminal only after he has been convicted of a much lesser offence?" ("Changes in trial rules urged" *The Independent* 28.5.91)

In other parts of Europe the practice varies. Cyprus and the Republic of Ireland hold to the same principle as the United Kingdom that criminal records can only be communicated to the court after guilt has been established, but in Austria, Denmark, Greece, Italy, Norway, Sweden and Turkey they may be read out during the trial (see Council of Europe 1984: 25-26).

In the UK the principle at present still stands and a number of case judgements have upheld it (see eg. Rv. Cohen (1984) 3 Cr App R (s) 300).

If a disclosure is made during a hearing a judge must caution a jury against what they have heard and try to ensure its exclusion from their judgement (see eg. Silcott 1987 CLR 765). A magistrate should exclude him or herself from sitting if they have heard a criminal record during proceedings and should only continue if the accused has no objections (R v Birmingham City Justices ex p Robinson 1986 150 JP 1), and the clerk has been notified that a conviction history has been revealed (R v. Downham Market Justices ex p Nudd 1988 152 JP 511). If the magistrate is sitting in a small town where certain residents are 'well known' it has been ruled that a magistrate may still hear the case (Rv. Metropolitan Stipendiary Magistrate ex p. Gallagher 1972 136 JPN 80). The rule against disclosure is also relaxed if proving the current charge relies on proof of earlier convictions (Rv Hall 1983 1 WLR 350 CA).

Moving from the finding of guilt to the sentencing decision we enter the realms of sentencing theory. It is beyond our present brief to look at various theories of sentencing in any depth and the reader is referred to other writers for such analysis (see eg. Walker 1985, von Hirsch 1986 or Wasik and Pease 1987). It is, however, important to the present thesis to consider the position and influence of a criminal record on sentencing.

In essence sentencers will be considering the immediate past behaviour of the offender that has resulted in his court appearance, and the likely future behaviour of the offender in terms of possible harm to the community and amenability to processes of 'treatment' or 'rehabilitation'. In weighing these 'just desserts' for past crimes alongside possible risks of future crimes the sentencer will be considering the part played by previous convictions. In practice over periods of time theories of sentencing have swung between favouring one school of thought over another. The eighties, for example, saw a resurgence of 'just deserts' and justice over treatment and welfare orientations.

A strict reading of the principle of 'just deserts' applied to sentencing might suggest that previous convictions had no part to play in sentencing decisions. A person is sentenced only for the crimes he has been convicted of in the present court hearing. The English Court of Appeal has stated the case that "even when a man has got a long record of crimes he must be sentenced for the offence he has committed" (Lawton L.J. in R V. Galloway 1979 Cr App R (s) 311). The common law position that a person cannot be sentenced twice for the same offence would appear to rule out any reference to past convictions. The 1991 Criminal Justice Act has put the position on to a statutory basis:

"An offence shall not be regarded as more serious for the purposes of any provision of this part by reason of any previous convictions of the offender or any failure of his to respond to previous sentences".

(Criminal Justice Act 1991 s.29(1))

The 1991 Act also repealed old legislation which had permitted 'extended sentences' for people with previous convictions meeting certain criteria (Powers of Criminal Courts Act 1973 s.28) and custodial sentences for young people who had failed to respond to non-custodial sentences (Criminal Justice Act 1982 s1 (4A)(a)). There is a clear understanding that a 'principle of proportionality' is applicable that makes the sentence proportionate to the crime committed; it is the crime that is being adjudged rather than the criminal.

Running parallel to the 'principle of proportionality', however, is the equally long standing principle of 'progressive' mitigation; whereby a first offender is entitled to a reduction in sentence from a maximum ceiling for the offence committed. In the event of subsequent offending there is a progressive loss of that entitlement to reduction until ultimately the offender receives the full proportionate sentence. Clearly there is a role here for the previous criminal convictions record to play a part in the sentencing process, and the record makes its entry into proceedings, following a conviction, in the form of ante-cedents reports and pre-sentence reports. The UK Criminal Justice Act 1991 qualifies its Section 29(1) with reference to courts being able to take into account "the circumstances of other offences committed by the offender" (s.29(2)).

Sentencing judgements are clearly to be made not only with reference to the crime but also to the criminal. As von Hirsh puts it, "the primary focus is on the present act, because the actor is being censured for his conduct. Any such censure, however, entails disapprobation directed at the actor himself" (von Hirsh 1986: 83).

The 'principle of proportionality' has also been breached by common law if there has been a public interest to do so. Such a public interest has been identified as including the incarceration of so-called 'dangerous' people when there is an accumulation of offences that seem to indicate the need for such a sentence (R.v. Gouws (1981) 3 Cr App R (s) 325). The Criminal Justice Act 1991 has put this assessment of risk and possible future harm to the community on to the UK statute book. Custodial sentences can also be passed on those who have specifically committed violent or sexual offences and who pose a risk of 'serious harm' to the public (s 1 (2)(b)). Before doing so a court must consider a pre-sentence report and other information available to it (s 3).

The onus is on those who have prosecuted a defendant to call for the convicted persons antecedents, in the 'public interest'. Antecedent reports consist of a statement identifying the person concerned together with his or her criminal conviction record. The court itself may call for other social inquiry or pre-sentence reports.

In a magistrates court the antecedents report is read aloud with some discretion being used on the inclusion of every conviction and with some being deemed less relevant (see Practice Directions 1975 1 WLR 1065). If the conviction puts the person in breach of an earlier sentence, such as a suspended sentence, that must be clearly put to the court. In a youth court care should be taken to separate out cautions from convictions to avoid "confusion between a caution and a previous finding of guilt" (Home Office 1978: para 3). A confusion that might increase in probability with the proposed merger of caution records into the mainstream of the national criminal record system (Home Office 1991: para 82).

As the criminal record was just one piece of information gathered in the search made by the investigating police officer in making his or her decision, so too it is just one piece of information in the sentencers search before making a decision. It has been estimated that up to 26 separate categories of information might be available to a sentencer, with some being more relevant than others (see Lloyd-Bostock 1988: 71). Of these the seriousness of the offence and previous convictions are of critical importance. In particular:

> "Prior record provides information on how set the offender is on a criminal career. This may lead to a moral judgement that the individual is more (or less) wicked, and hence deserving of a more (or less) severe sentence".
>
> (Lloyd-Bostock 1988: 73)

The result is described by Lloyd-Bostock as an 'attributional model' of sentencing where those with a previous record are seen as more career criminals and therefore more responsible than those with no previous record. In practice this is carried through procedurally to complement the 'principle of proportionality' and taken into account as aggravating or mitigating circumstances.

In practice sentencers will consider the number of previous convictions in the criminal record and their seriousness and the seriousness with which they have been assessed by other courts. The frequency of former offending and the existence of 'conviction free' gaps in the record will be weighed as will the similarity between the current offence and previous offences. Note will also be taken of the age of the person at the time of the earlier convictions and the degree of compliance that was achieved in serving previous sentences. Finally sentencers may be expected to consider the 'staleness' of old convictions in much the same way as the UK Rehabilitation of Offenders Act 1974 allows old convictions to become 'spent' (see Wasik 1987 for a lengthier discussion of these factors).

The quality of criminal records and their accuracy is critical to the integrity of antecedent reports and their use in making sentencing decisions. In the UK the Law Society has stated its findings that in fact records are "in a terrifying condition of inaccuracy" (House of Commons 1990 (a): para 1). At the time of writing the Government has put its faith in increased computerisation to improve the accuracy of criminal records (Home Office 1990(a)) and disputed records can be checked manually with clerks to courts (see eg. Magistrates Courts Rules 1981 rule 68).

Criminal courts may call for the writing of social inquiry reports which were re-named as pre-sentence reports by the Criminal Justice Act 1991. In essence their purpose is to inform the decision making of sentencets, make recommendations as to how a criminal career might be checked and advise on the likely effect of a specific form of sentence. The writers of these reports have access to previous conviction records, and are asked to place them in context alongside such factors as the defendants family background, health and education. Evidence exists that the Probation Service have experienced difficulty in getting access to records for reports, and have sometimes had to resort to "relying on the defendant to provide an account of any previous record" (Home Office 1991: para 19).

The Home Office and Lord Chancellors office set out the requirements of social inquiry reports in the 1961 Streatfield Report (Home Office/Lord Chancellor's Office 1961). Subsequent guidance has always confirmed a need to provide adequate interpretation or comment on the criminal history of a defendant (Home Office 1986(d)), culminating in the 1990 requirement to include information about the offence, the offenders attitude to it and other background information on the offender (Home Office 1990(d): 12-13). Following the passage of the Criminal Justice Act 1991 the Home Office began drafting new guidelines on the content of pre-sentence reports and how to present the 'circumstances' of previous convictions.

On juvenile offenders the Department of Health has offered similar guidance to local authority social workers presenting reports to the youth court. Advice is given on how to place a criminal record in a social context by reference to the number of offences, intervals between offences, and previous disposals and their effectiveness (DHSS 1987: para 108). Home Office guidance to the police on the disclosure of criminal records for purposes of writing reports in both criminal and civil proceedings is contained in Circular 54/1986 (Home Office 1986 (a): Annex A Schedule 1).

A court can also request medical and psychiatric reports and these too may make references to criminal records even though there appears to be no direct disclosure mechanisms that include the medical practitioner.

The Mental Health Act 1983 s.37 permits a court to sentence a convicted person to be compulsorily detained in a hospital or be the subject of a Guardianship Order. In addition a magistrates court has powers to make such orders without recording a conviction (s.37(3)) and "where a conviction would prove stigmatising" (Gostin 1984: 33; see also Home Office 1990(e)). These provisions are aimed at the temporarily ill, people with learning difficulties or mental impairment and those who have committed minor offences.

Researchers into the nature of the sentencing process and the qualities of sentences have described how frames of reference are built up by sentencers to assess situations in what is an 'open-problem' solving task. In other words a problem without clear, unambiguous criteria for a correct solution. In making the decision sentencers will take into account a criminal record and pre-sentence reports and also need to be aware of making automatic responses as opposed to more considered responses and of making sentences in the context of a given tariff of sentences available and as matched against the individual before them in the court. The sentencer will also have his or her own prejudices and point of view to bring to the decision making (see Lloyd-Bostock 1988).

The press, the public and the court

An essential feature of courts administering justice is held to be their openness to public scrutiny. Public galleries allow people to witness proceedings and ensure 'justice is seen to be done'. More often the public gain their information from press reporting of court hearings. Apart from ensuring that the due process of law has been carried out fairly, the press reporting of court hearings carries with it the scope for public opinion to be passed on the convicted person, including the public 'shaming' of that person:

> "Some defendants actually give as a reason for pleading guilty or not choosing trial the fear that they would run the risk of attracting more publicity if they did anything other than plead guilty in the magistrates court". (King 1981: 95)

Legal safeguards often preclude the reporting of hearings involving juveniles or sexual offenders and their victims, and it is generally held that the press should not disclose previous convictions, if known, during a trial for the same reasons the court itself would not disclose it.

In 1989 in the UK the Home Office agreed procedures with justices clerks on making information available to the media from a court. This information was to include lists available on the day of a hearing but also the possibility that courts should allow media access to the court register in which the courts decisions are recorded. The latter would allow local newspapers in particular to waive their right to see justice being done, but ensure that the publicity attendant upon a conviction was still maintained. The result has been the listing in local newspapers of little more than names, addresses and nature of conviction of local people with only a select few having their cases fully reported (see Home Office 1989a).

At the end of a court hearing and over the subsequent months and years, the nature of a conviction moves from one of open record to one of a closed record. Although most criminal justice systems recognise such a move when a curtain descends, "at the moment of conviction and sentence or the day after" (Adelman 1990: 22) this shift from open to closed record keeping has been questioned.

In the USA the argument was put by journalists that having once been public a record of a court conviction did not necessarily remove itself from the public domain once it went from the court into a repository. Using the federal Freedom of Information Act a CBS reporter tried to obtain the criminal record of a Rhode Island family with an alleged history of organised crime. The 'public records should be public' argument was countered successfully in the case of Reporters Committee for Freedom of the Press v. US Department of Justice. It was held that at the point of entry to the judicial system, an openness to scrutiny was required to ensure justice but such openness, hereafter, was not required when a conviction became part of a non-public compilation of records.

In the UK the Rehabilitation of Offenders Act 1974 is applicable to press reporting and prohibits the publication of 'spent offences' as an unauthorised disclosure that could give grounds for an action of defamation. People in positions of authorised access to criminal records would be committing an offence by disclosure "in response to 'fishing' enquiries from the press or members of the public", (Home Office 1975: para 6). Most other European countries have forms of rehabilitation procedures that either automatically operate, as in Belgium, Germany or France, after a given time, or are made by an administrative decision such as Norway or Spain (see Breed n.d: chapter 7).

The Council of Europe has encouraged its member states to ensure close cooperation between judicial authorities and the press to see that criminal records are not indiscriminately published and the rights of individuals to a degree of privacy are maintained where possible. The Council was anxious not to infringe upon the right to freedom of expression. (Council of Europe 1984: para 11 (7))

In the UK the press has sought to regulate itself through first the Press Council and later its successor the Press Complaints Commission. An essential part of the process of regulation concerned the maintenance of peoples privacy which should not be intruded upon unless clearly in the public interest. The question of privacy and the press had been explored in some depth by the 1990 Calcutt Report which had drawn up a draft Code of Practice as part of its submission in favour of self-regulation. Paragraph 14 of the draft ruled that even where the law did not prohibit it "an individuals criminal convictions should not be published unless the reference to them is directly relevant to the matter reported." (Home Office 1990(f): 123). Unfortunately this provision has been dropped from the resulting Code of Practice adopted by the Press Complaints Commission.

Post-Court

At the point of sentence and departure from a court, various receiving agencies of the penal system will also receive criminal records and social inquiry/pre-sentence reports along with the convicted person. These will include in the UK, prisons, young offender institutes and attendance centres.

In the USA states vary in their willingness to similarly make records available some of them preferring to abide by the principle of a 'demonstrated need' for the records. (Barton 1990: 28)

Local authorities in the UK may also act as an adjunct to the criminal justice and penal system in receiving criminal records on certain people at the end of a custodial sentence. This practice particularly applies to people convicted of offences against children and Home Office guidance places the Probation Service as the intermediary agency between prisons, young offender institutions and local authorities. The purpose of the arrangements is to ensure the safety of children who may be present at any address the discharged prisoner may be going to live at. The local authority is charged with making a prior visit to the address to discuss the welfare of children who may be 'at risk' of the former prisoner going to live there. (Home Office 1964: para 6: DHSS 1978).

These child protection arrangements have been criticised for only covering former prisoners and not people who receive non-custodial sentences (Kahan and Levy 1991: para 16-31; but also see Home Office 1964: para 7). They have also been criticised when they do not appear to have worked efficiently and children have been harmed as a result (London Boro. of Lambeth 1987: 152-3).

In practice an ex-prisoner has only to leave the address he was discharged to from prison, to create problems for child care agencies wishing to keep his whereabouts on record. The spectre of the constantly moving ex-offender with a record of convictions against children tests our belief in liberal democracy and the limits of social control mechanisms we are willing to enter into. Some local authorities we know have created their own informal 'criminal record offices' consisting of people in their area known to have a record of offences against children (see Dept. of Health 1991a: para 6.52). The Children Act 1989 both places a duty on local authorities to apply for orders removing children from households where they might be 'at risk' (s.31 and s.44) and gives a power to authorities to financially assist an alleged abuser to leave a household where children may be endangered (Schedule 2 para.5), (see also chapter 6).

5 Criminal records – Disclosure and vetting

Introduction

In the previous chapter we detailed and examined the use of criminal records for what is usually regarded as their primary purpose – namely, as an adjunct to the workings of the criminal justice system. However, as mentioned in our introduction in chapter 1, criminal records can be viewed as having several purposes. Here we examine their disclosure and use outside the criminal justice system. This chapter explores disclosure from a comparative perspective, looking at the situation in the UK and USA.

The UK

While in chapter 3 we saw that the existence and coverage of the national collection of criminal records is acknowledged in legislation – the *purpose* of the records, and the detail of what each record is to contain is not prescribed in law. In the words of a recent Home Office report:

> "The systems have grown up over time to fulfil needs seen by the police and by some other customers." (Home Office 1991: 4)

Disclosure as understood in the UK has taken two forms: first, police reporting of convictions to employers in certain regulated employments and second, in vetting which provides access to the criminal record prior to or in connection with an employment decision.

This chapter sets out to examine arrangements for disclosure outside of the strictly judicial or criminal justice purpose, and it looks at the development of such arrangements in the UK and USA. Where research material has allowed, the chapter also references the state of disclosure in certain European countries. A number of issues are pertinent to an adequate analysis of this vetting purpose, and we conclude with an examination of the impact of such disclosure for concepts of rehabilitation and the possibilities for the amplification of effects of an already discriminatory justice system.

Development of disclosure in the UK

As pointed out in an earlier chapter, since the repeal in 1967 of the Prevention of Crimes Act (1871), there has not existed a statutory authority on the police to maintain a national system of criminal records (albeit that there are now regulations governing recording of certain offences in national records under the 1984 Police and Criminal Evidence Act). This being so, it is not until the Rehabilitation of Offenders Act 1974 that we find some formal recognition of police records when there is reference to the concept of disclosure of 'official record' – namely:

> "A record kept by...any police force...being a record containing information about persons convicted of offences."
>
> (Rehabilitation of Offenders Act 1974, s9 (11))

However, it has long been accepted that records would be kept by the police and that the decision to disclose information in police possession, of which the 'criminal record' forms a part, rests with the chief officer of the force (chief constable). Again, as mentioned in an earlier chapter, this line of reasoning is in keeping with the present interpretation of police governance in the UK which stresses the historical independence of the police from the executive (Government) and the particular notion of the 'office of constable' with its accountability solely to the law (but for an alternative account of police history and governance see Lustgarten 1986).

It is possible to trace the current basis of disclosure of criminal records through a series of circulars issued to chief officers of police by the Home Office. Before describing this process, it is worth noting that the status of government circulars is complex (see Ganz 1987 for a full exploration of the intricacies) but one interpretation is that such quasi-legislation should be seen as government by informal rules. It has been suggested that:

> "One view of such 'rules' is that they offer a useful structuring of discretion: another is that they are often used cynically so as to make law without resort to Parliament, to instruct judges on the meaning of statutes and to insulate bureaucracies from review."   (Baldwin and Houghton 1986: 239)

Lustgarten describes the use of circulars as: "...a form of regulation in public law which deserves more study than it has received, which because it is not technically subordinate legislation, receives no Parliamentary scrutiny." (Lustgarten ibid: 105).

Government departmental circulars, such as those issued by the Home Office to the police, are in essence guidance. This guidance emerges as a result of a consultation process involving Home Office officials and the Association of Chief Police Officers (ACPO) (representing the police service at its highest levels). But in the final analysis, the only constraints on the individual chief constable's discretion to disclose are those legal provisions of the 1984 Data Protection Act which prevent the disclosure of information held on computer other than in accordance with registration of the computer system. Under the 1984 Act, the chief police officers of England, Wales and Scotland are the registered 'data users' or more colloquially the 'owners' of the records. The data users who control the contents and use of personal data are obliged to place details of that use in a public register. They are also required to follow the good practices described in a series of principles (the Data Protection Principles). The Third Principle states that personal data held for any purpose or purposes shall not be used or disclosed in any manner incompatible with that purpose or those purposes. In essence the Act does not prevent additional uses being made of criminal records held for policing purposes. The interpretation of the Third Principle effectively allows additional uses as long as they are registered (see the Memorandum of Evidence by the Data Protection Registrar to the House of Commons Home Affairs Committee *Criminal Records* Third Report Session 1989-90, HMSO). The terms of police forces' standard registration under the 1984 Data Protection Act of their respective sets of records held on the PNC is treated as providing a bureau service to forces. The general purposes for which data are held in police record systems are listed as the prevention and detection of crime; apprehension and prosecution of offenders; protection of life and property; maintenance of law and order; and rendering assistance to the public. Within that, the registration lists the individuals or organizations to whom the content of the record may be disclosed. The current list, and we trace development of this disclosure list later in the chapter, includes all Government departments, a number of other public sector bodies, some former public sector bodies such as British Telecom, local authorities and 'authorities and organizations connected with the care/supervision of those who are deemed vulnerable e.g. the young, handicapped or infirm'. The terms of the registration make it clear that the examples are not intended to be an exhaustive list of categories of disclosure. The 1984 Data Protection Act only applies to those records held on computer (or more accurately, those 'automatically processed'), however, as was pointed out in chapter 3, most police forces also hold local manually indexed criminal information systems, and these are not covered by the Act.

We have elsewhere reviewed the background to police disclosure in the UK (Thomas and Hebenton 1991a), but in what follows we seek to widen and deepen that background and to examine more thoroughly the nature of current arrangements.

It is possible to trace a number of circulars, issued over the last 70 years, to chief officers of police by the Home Office on the subject of information disclosure from records. In the period from 1925 until 1955, we have located the following: Home Office consolidated circular on crime, 1 January 1925; circulars 16 January 1926; 12 September 1933; No.126/1944; No.160/1944; No.56/1945; No.54/1951; No.151/1954. All these circulars dealt with either police reports of convictions in relation to certain occupations or police reports on character of candidates for certain types of employment. It is clear that by 1954 vetting had become established in principle as a proper, if limited, extension of the original police purpose of the criminal record. Vetting was seen not as an exception to the record's confidentiality, but rather as an extension of police use of it for the prevention of crime. Home Office Circular No. 151/1954 *Reports of Convictions of Teachers*, for example, emerged as a result of Parliamentary concern over homosexual offences and recent cases in which people convicted of offences against children had been found to be employed in private (independent) schools (for an interesting discussion of the concern see Public Record Office HO 287/251 Minutes of Meeting of Central Conference of Chief Constables on 25th February 1954). The No.151/1954 circular asked chief constables to report the conviction of any person who is:

"a. a teacher in any type of school;

b. a person employed in the care of children (including the resident proprietor of a private school), in a residential school, remand home, approved school, children's home, approved probation hostel or approved probation home;

c. a youth leader;

d. a minister of any religious denomination if he or she is convicted of any offence which, in your opinion, renders him or her unsuitable to be employed in teaching or in the care of children".

The circular also pointed out to chief officers that relevant government departments had agreed to indemnify the police against liability on any civil claim against the police as a result of supplying a report of conviction.

Consistent with this general approach, in 1954 the final report of the Working Party on Police Reports, which had been established by the Central Conference of Chief Constables in 1952 identified two principles which should guide disclosure of the criminal record for vetting purposes. These were:

a.   that police information should not be used except for the purposes of which it was acquired, and therefore it should not be disclosed to persons in authority, however responsible, other than those concerned with police functions, unless the consideration of public interest was sufficiently weighty to justify departure from the general rule; and

b.   that a person who had served his sentence or otherwise paid the penalty for his crime should not, by official action, be placed in the position where he found it impossible to rehabilitate himself and build a new and honest life.

The recommendations of the Working Party's final report were produced as guidance under Home Office circular No.77/1955 *Police Reports for Government Departments and Other Authorities*, issued on 2 May 1955. This circular replaced previous guidance and in particular revised the list of reports of convictions and reports on character to be furnished by chief constables. The previous list of reports as contained in the Home Office consolidated circular of 1 January 1925 was thus replaced.

Chief constables under the terms of circular No.77/1955 were asked to furnish to the Home Office or various employing bodies, as a matter of routine, reports of convictions of people in the following categories:

a.   pensioners and widows of pensioners of the Royal Irish Constabulary

b.   registered medical practitioners

c.   registered dental practitioners

d.   state certified midwives

e.   state registered nurses, enrolled nurses, student nurses, pupil assistant nurses

f.   teachers and others having the care of children

g.   justices of the peace

h.   drivers of public service vehicles

i.   holders of air crew licences

j.   solicitors' or solicitors' clerks.

In relation to reports on character, circular No.77/1955 invited chief constables to furnish, if requested to do so, reports in respect of:

a.   candidates for the Admiralty Constabulary

b.   candidates for the corps of the Royal Military Police, the Military Provost staff corps, the War Department Constabulary

c.   candidates for the Air Ministry Constabulary and airmen selected for the Royal Air Force Police

d.   candidates for casual employment with the Post Office at Christmas who are not already known to the Head Postmaster

e.   Royal Irish Constabulary pensioners who wish to commute their pensions.

A number of subsequent circulars followed (No.206/1955; No.66/1958; No.11/1961; No.41/1963; No.6/1964; No.4/1969) but in 1972 concern was expressed in Parliament about the lack of openness with respect to police instructions on disclosing information from criminal records. Accordingly, a joint Home Office and ACPO working party was established to review arrangements. The conclusions and recommendations of the working party were made known in a statement to the House of Commons by the then Home Secretary Robert Carr (see *Hansard*, 14 June 1973, cols 1680-1682). Carr restated the general principle that police information would not be given to anyone, however responsible, unless there were weighty considerations of public interest which justified departure from the general rule. He outlined general grounds for disclosure, consistent with earlier principles given in the 1954 report: namely,

-    the protection of vulnerable members of society

-    national security

-    the need to ensure probity in the administration of the law.

The circular incorporating these recommendations was issued on 13 August 1973, as circular No.140/1973. In relation to reports of convictions this now added barristers to the list, and reports on character were reviewed and amended to contain:

a. prospective adoptive and foster parents

b. applicants for criminal injury compensation

c. applicants to join the police (including Ministry of Defence, Airport, Docks and Transport police)

d. applicants for certificates under the 1968 Gaming Act

e. applicants for and holders of licences as Heavy Goods Vehicles and Passenger Service Vehicle Operators

f. applicants for licences as dealers in securities

g. applicants for various licences, certifications, registrations, dealt with locally under other statutory procedures.

Interestingly, the Home Secretary acknowledged in his June 1973 statement to Parliament that he considered it right for the police to maintain the practice, which did not have statutory authority, of helping Children's Departments in considering applications for prospective adoptive and foster parents, of checking the background of those wishing to join police forces and of those seeking financial compensation from the Criminal Injuries Compensation Board.

Since the issue of circular No.140/1973, however, there has been continuing pressure to extend areas of disclosure in relation to children and the elderly, often as a result of specific incidents. For example, in 1982 it was agreed that information on convictions should be disclosed to local authority social services departments in respect of applicants seeking registration as childminders (circular No. 105/1982).

The single largest increase in disclosure arrangements came with the issuing of circular No. 44/1986, *Protection of children: disclosure of criminal background of those with access to children*. The background to the issuing of this circular and its procedural provisions are dealt with in detail in the next chapter, but here it is sufficient to note that the circular introduced new arrangements in relation to local authority paid staff or volunteers who applied to or transferred to work with children. The circular set out an illustrative list of the main groups for whom police checks should be requested –however, it was the responsibility of the local authority to determine whether a particular job involved 'substantial access'. The main groups indicated were:

90

a.   prospective long-term and short-term foster parents (including private foster parents), and other adults in their households

b.   prospective adoptive parents, and other adults in their households

c.   applicants for custodianship orders, and other adults in their households

d.   childminders on registration, and other adults in their household

e.   staff of local authority-provided day nurseries and similar local authority facilities

f.   managers and staff in community (children's) homes provided by local authorities and controlled community homes

g.   local authority social services staff and other local authority departmental staff who have substantial opportunity for access to children

h.   school teachers in maintained schools

i.   professional staff in education departments (e.g. educational psychologists)

j.   other people working on or from school or other local authority premises and whose work brings them regularly into contact with children (e.g. school bus drivers, caretakers)

k.   youth workers

l.   probation officers and probation service staff who have substantial opportunity for access to children

m.   volunteers working for authorities in the above areas.

The provisions of this circular were subsequently revised by circular No.102/1988 which, among other things, provided greater clarity as to the posts which should be checked against police criminal records.

In the light of similar concerns about the welfare of the elderly, an amendment was agreed to the 1984 Registered Homes Act which now provides for disclosure. The procedural arrangements were set out in Home Office circular No.22/1991 *Disclosure of criminal background: proprietors and managers of residential care homes and nursing homes*.

The most recent area of disclosure relates to the licensing of taxi-drivers. In the UK there are essentially two types of 'taxi'– the black-cab or hackney carriage which is permitted to pick-up and set-down anywhere, and the private-hire vehicle which must be 'booked' by prior arrangement. Although local authorities who are responsible for issuing 'taxi' licences could under the 1976 Local Government (Miscellaneous Provisions) Act request applicants to declare any previous convictions, they had no independent means via a request for police disclosure of the criminal record of establishing the truth or otherwise of this declaration. Following heated controversy about alleged sexual assaults on women passengers, the government provided a statutory provision for such a police check. An amendment to the 1976 Act was made under s.47 of the 1991 Road Traffic Act:

> "For the purpose of satisfying themselves as to whether an applicant is a fit and proper person to hold a driver's licence, a council may send to the chief officer of police for the police area in which the council is situated –
>
> (a) a copy of that person's application, and
>
> (b) a request for the chief officer's observations; and the chief officer shall respond to the request".

The provisions of the related Home Office circular No.13/1992 came into effect on 1 April 1992.

All previous circular guidance was consolidated and superseded by the Home Office circular to chief officers of police No.45/1986 *Police reports of convictions and related information*. This circular, yet to be amended in light of the latest disclosure developments, lists as a schedule the groups on whom reports of convictions should be sent to appropriate authorities. New groups added since the 1973 listing include:

a.   civil servants (including prison officers and all other prison service employees)

b.   staff of the UK Atomic Energy Authority and British Nuclear Fuels

c.   British Telecom staff

d.   Post Office staff

e.   Civil Aviation Authority staff

f.   pharmaceutical chemists.

In relation to reports on character, the circular No.45/1986 has the following additions:

a.   those about to be appointed to positions giving substantial access to children

b.   persons involved in the care of (or as a member of the same household as) a child subject to a case conference on non-accidental injury to children

c.   parents (and their cohabitees) to whom a local authority proposes to return a child in care

d.   applicants for certificates under the 1976 Lotteries and Amusements Act

e.   applicants for consumer credit licences

f.   applicants for sex establishment and entertainment licences

g.   applicants for casual post office work

h.   potential jurors in cases including national security and terrorism

i.   social enquiry reports and other reports by probation officers to Crown Courts and magistrates' courts

j.   welfare reports for courts determining care and custody of children

k.   parties to divorce under Rule 10 of the Matrimonial Causes Rules 1977.

Before concluding this section, it is interesting to note the use, not listed in the circular, of police reports on visitors to convicted 'category A' prisoners. Under prison standing orders such prisoners are required to submit lists of their prospective visitors for checking by the police, and the visitors must supply photographs of themselves as an aid to identification. The justification of these requirements is to prevent such prisoners from arranging to be visited by other professional criminals. In essence, the police check the *bona fides* of a proposed visitor, establish whether he has a criminal record, verify his address and authenticate his photographs.

Disclosure and vetting – below the surface

The extent of and the nature of disclosure arrangements has traditionally been shrouded in the 'fog of administrative bureaucracy'. James Rule, writing of his experience in the early 1970s of research on criminal records, points out the obfuscation and denial of the extent of disclosure:

> "Specifically, when questioned about the provision of criminal record data to government agencies, one of the (Home Office) officials denied that such provision occurs, except 'very rarely' and 'under exceptional circumstances', circumstances which he declined to explain. And yet, standing instructions from the Home Office Police Department require local police forces to communicate as a matter of course the details of convictions of members of broad categories of the British populace".
>
> (Rule 1973: 79)

In the UK, the first real public examination of the issue of disclosure came with the inquiry by the House of Commons Home Affairs Select Committee into the maintenance and use of criminal records (see previous discussions of the Committee's report in chapter 3) which was published in April 1990 (House of Commons 1990a). The Home Office, in its memorandum of evidence to the Committee pointed out that the number of government vetting searches of the criminal record had grown from 377,639 in 1986 to 508,942 in 1989 (House of Commons 1990a: 2). This figure of over 500,000 inquiries was referred to as 'remarkable' by a member of the Committee, who then proceeded to ask a summoned witness, the Head of the Science and Technology Group of the Home Office Police Department, why the number had risen so dramatically.

In reply, it was stated:

"Government searches are carried out on civil servants and other casual staff and contractors, consultants, and so on, who might have access to classified material as part of their duties".

(House of Commons 1990a: 15)

In their written report, the Committee dealt with this response head on:

" Mr. Hughes of the Home Office said that these searches were carried out 'for the protection of national security. They are not carried out on all civil servants, they are only carried out on those who might have access to classified material. So it is restricted.'. We are surprised, given the restricted conditions under which searches are said to occur, that 508,942 took place in 1989. Assuming that each search was on a different person, it means that about 1 per cent of the adult population of the United Kingdom was checked in that one year. We find it hard to believe that over half a million people were taken into Government employment directly or indirectly in 1989 who had access to 'classified material' to the extent that revealing it would harm national security ".

(House of Commons 1990a: viii)

In addition to considering government vetting, the Home Affairs Committee also commented on the arrangements covered by the circulars referred to earlier in this chapter. Such disclosure raised three questions argued the Committee

- to whom should criminal records be available?
- what information is available?
- how can it be ensured that a record relates to the 'right' person?

On the first question, the report points out that although they did not take evidence on the appropriateness or otherwise of current disclosure categories, the Committee were of the opinion that current arrangements do not provide a satisfactory mechanism for making criminal records available. The report notes and agrees with the view of the UK Data Protection Registrar that present arrangements place chief police officers in a difficult position, being subject to pressure in deciding what are effectively matters of broader public interest. The report continues:

> "The fact that 51 police forces might permit access in a haphazard and unaccountable manner has worrying implications for the liberty of the individual. We believe that if the public were more aware of these arrangements, there would be an outcry. There is no element of accountability in the present arrangements and no guarantee of national consistency". (House of Commons 1990a: ix)"

The Committee also considered the question of the nature of the information made available on disclosure, and were concerned that it could include not only convictions, but also police 'intelligence'. On the third matter of correct 'matching' of record to person, the Committee were informed by the Commander of the NIB that there could be no certainty in the absence of a requirement for fingerprints.

The Home Affairs Committee concluded that present disclosure arrangements do not provide satisfactory answers to any of the three questions posed. The report's recommendations on disclosure and the government's response are dealt with in the final chapter. Before leaving this section on disclosure arrangements in the UK, however, it is worth noting the peculiar role of a further legislative device.

The 1974 Rehabilitation of Offenders Act and its exceptions – the UK's alternative vetting strategy?

In the early 1970s, at the same time as disclosure of records was beginning to become more comprehensive and more widely acknowledged, there was also Parliamentary consideration of the need to produce legislation that would remove an ex-offender's conviction after a number of years providing no other offence had been committed. A number of countries already had legislation by then, including the USA and Canada. Eventually in 1973 a private Member's bill, taking forward the recommendations of the Gardiner committee report *Living It Down* was introduced to Parliament. The resulting Rehabilitation of Offenders Act 1974 has been described as:

"an extremely clumsy piece of legislation, both difficult to understand and to use". (Breed n.d.: 16)

However, it was an achievement. In its simplest terms it meant that any person who had been convicted of a criminal offence and who had not been sentenced to more than 30 months in prison would automatically become a 'rehabilitated person'. Providing that no other indictable offence was committed during the 'rehabilitation period', the conviction would be regarded as 'spent'. When applying for jobs, the conviction would not need to be disclosed, nor could the conviction be used as a reason for refusing employment (see Thomson 1982 for a detailed discussion of the UK legal position). In relation to the concerns of this book, however, it is not so much the badly drafted provisions of the Act as the subsequent exceptions to it that are of importance. When one examines the Parliamentary debates about the need for exceptions to the Act (*Hansard* (Commons) Session 1974-5 894, cols 169-197) discussion is dominated by appeals to 'common-sense'. The term 'common-sense' is used over and again by both government ministers and others in looking at which occupations should be exempt. The range of applicants for exception in 1975 has only recently been revealed and further illustrates the wide ranging nature of who properly considered themselves outside the provisions of the Rehabilitation of Offenders Act (see figure 9).

The details of the agreed exceptions were given in the Rehabilitation of Offenders Act 1974 (Exceptions) Order 1975, SI 1975 No. 1023. This list of exceptions, together with the further amendments of 1986 (SI 1986 Nos. 1249 and 2268) are given in the Annex (reproduced from *The National Collection of Criminal Records* Report of an Efficiency Scrutiny, Home Office 1991). The effect of an exception is that an applicant for any job within the areas specified must if asked quote all his or her previous convictions, including 'spent' convictions. What is apparent, is that an examination of the range of posts subject to exceptions is wider than those subject to disclosure vetting. As the Annex shows, 23 of the 49 categories of exception would probably not allow police disclosure of the criminal record. This would tend to suggest that exceptions to the 1974 Act have been granted as an alternative to police disclosure.

Figure 9

The Association of British Adoption Agencies
The National Deaf Children's Society
The National Council for Social Services
The National Association for Deaf/Blind and Rubella Children
The National Society for Mentally Handicapped Children
The Ockenden Venture
The NSPCC
The Church of England Children's Society
The Girl Guides Association
The National Institute for the Deaf
The National Council of Voluntary Child Care Organisations
The National Association of Boys Clubs
The Church Army
The National Association of Youth Clubs
The General Synod Board of Education
Christians Abroad
The Baden Powell Scout's Association
The Scout Association
The Methodist Church Division of Education and Youth
The Local Authority Associations (and individual local authorities)
The GLC and ILEA
The General Medical Council
The General Dental Council
The General Nursing Council
The Central Midwives Board
The General Optical Council
The Pharmaceutical Society of Great Britain
The Royal College of Veterinary Surgeons
The Law Society
The Senate of the Inns of Court and the Bar
The Architects Registration Council of the United Kingdom
The Institute of Chartered Accountants in England and Wales
The Royal Institution of Chartered Surveyors
The Police
The British Bankers Association
The London Diamond Bourse
The Committee of Magistrates for Inner London
The Fire Service
Representatives of the Press
The Bank of England
The Retail Distributors Association Incorporated
Augustus Barnett and Sons Ltd.
The Museums Association
The London Diamond Club Ltd.
The National Supervisory Council for Intruder Alarms Ltd.
The British Security Industries Association
The National Freight Corporation
The Association of British Investigators
The British Shipping Federation
The British Casino Association
The Betting Office Licensees Association
The British Bingo Association
The National Association of Licensed Bingo and Social Clubs
The Continental Oil Company Ltd.
Johnson, Matthey and Co. Ltd.
The Accepting Houses Committee
The British Jewellery and Giftware Federation Ltd.
The Wellcome Foundation Ltd.
Members of the London Gold Market
The British Museum
The Civil Aviation Authority
The British Insurance Association and Lloyds
The Royal Commission on Historical Monuments

Hansard March 27, 1990. PQ (written) No. 141.

The USA

Introduction and definitions

As was pointed out in chapter 2, in the USA criminal history records, sometimes called 'rap sheets', are cumulative, name-indexed histories of an individual's involvement in the criminal justice system. As such, criminal history data invariably is the most useful and the easiest to use record of arrests and convictions; however, it is not the only such record of arrests and convictions. Two other kinds of criminal record information exist, both of which have traditionally been openly available to the public.

First, there is the police record of arrests and other information maintained daily at the police station. However, these so called 'blotters' or logs are usually not retrievable by name and only very rarely are cumulative – therefore they do not cross-reference and would require a search of all daily logs to obtain a picture of someone's previous criminal history. By statute or case law in most states, and as a sign of proper legislative working, these daily logs are open to public inspection.

Second, every US court keeps a record, usually called a docket, of events transpiring in the court that day. The docket is therefore a slice of judicial proceedings and includes details of sentences. In some courts these records are indexed by name and are cumulative – that is, all of the events in a given court, even events involving different cases, in which a particular individual participated can be checked by using that person's name; in addition, courts are also preparing these dockets for automatic processing. Historically, dockets have been regarded as open as a matter of constitutional right and usually backed by statute.

This section on disclosure in the USA sets out by examining the legal background and then reviews the evidence for the extent and growth of such arrangements over recent years. As with the UK material, the primary discussion of social and public policy implications is reserved to the concluding section to this chapter.

Disclosure – the legal context

As early as 1924, when the US Congress appropriated funds to the Justice Department for the collection of criminal records, the Congress established general standards for the disclosure of such information by authorizing " their exchange with the officials of States, cities and other institutions;..." (Pub.L. No. 68-153, 43 Stat. 205,217 (1924)). This position, subsequently amended in 1957 to permit the FBI to cancel the exchange of records if agencies disseminated records to a third party, meant that by the late 1950s records held at the federal level had already been made unavailable to the public.

However, the situation at state and local level did not have the same history.

While it could be pointed out that a 1984 survey had shown that nearly all states had established central criminal history repositories facilitating access to a complete record at a single source, and that the same report pointed out that most states has some sort of statutes addressing disclosure (SEARCH Group 1984), this had not always been the case.

The early state criminal history systems were created by the police for police purposes. Accordingly, decisions to create such records, maintain such records, use such records, or disclose such records were regarded as matters of exclusive police discretion. According to the US Department of Justice:

"Well into the mid-1960s, criminal history records in most states were exempt from open record or official record laws. A 1971 survey by a University of Chicago researcher found that, in general, arrest records were disclosed or, more often, withheld solely at police discretion: 'Courts usually refuse to interfere with the police practice of limiting public access to arrest records but circulating the records at their discretion.' Early court challenges to the selective release of criminal history data by police departments were rebuffed on the grounds that the records were not confidential at common law or by statute".

(US Department of Justice 1988: 4)

This position began to alter in the late 1960s. As we pointed out in chapter 1, this period of 'revolution' and mistrust of big government also saw a resurgence in interest in privacy rights and notions of confidentiality. By the early 1970s, the exercise of police discretion selectively to disclose criminal history records outside of the criminal justice system was under attack. The basis for the attack included concerns about the computerization of records, the potential for misuse, the poor quality of the records, and the unfairness to offenders arising from selective release of information, especially arrest data without a subsequent prosecution (see Gutman 1982 for a statement of the concerns on arrest data). These concerns created a climate in which selective and discretionary disclosure was now politically untenable. Westin and Baker (1972) provide an illustrative account of how the rules of the game were changing. In November 1970, a television reporter revealed that the police chief of Kansas City had obtained criminal record information from the city's computerized system and then passed it on to local businessmen and landlords. The purpose, according to the police department was to "keep an eye on who was coming into town" (Westin and Baker ibid: 87). When the media charged that, "for the computer data to be available to private interest suggest the 'Big

Brother' of Orwell's book..", the chief of police replied that "without the use of this computer these people would now be residents in our community." (Westin and Baker ibid: 87).

Out of that period came substantial reforms in the management of criminal history records in general and the disclosure of records in particular. In 1973, the US congress moved toward regulating disclosure policy and assuring that criminal history record information maintained in state and local information systems would be as unavailable to the public as those of the FBI. The Crime Control Act of 1973, amending the earlier 1968 Omnibus Crime Control and Safe Streets Act (sometimes referred to as the 'Kennedy Amendment'), required that all criminal history records in state and local systems that received federal funding should "only be used for law enforcement and criminal justice and other lawful purposes." (Pub. L. No.93-83, 87 Stat. 197, 215 (1973)).

The US Congress recognized the vague wording of limiting disclosure to "lawful purposes", and it held hearings on proposed criminal records bills throughout 1974 and 1975. This legislation, among other things, would have established a national standard for disclosure. However, as Belair (1988) points out none of these bills emerged from committee due, in some measure, to fierce opposition by the US newspapers.

Meanwhile the Project SEARCH Group, whose origins were referred to in chapter 2, supported the 1974 and 1975 legislation and at that time published its technical report on the need to adopt comprehensive model standards for state and local systems (SEARCH Group 1975). These standards, among other things, called for prohibiting public access to criminal history records except where access was required to comply with federal or state statute.

In 1976, the Law Enforcement Assistance Administration (LEAA) adopted comprehensive regulations for records. However, with respect to disclosure, the LEAA regulations took a middle ground - they did not restrict the disclosure of conviction record information and furthermore, even with respect to nonconviction arrest data, the regulations permit disclosure to any party, including the public when permitted by state or local law.

While the LEAA regulations and the SEARCH standards provided a much needed impetus, the courts were changing the law. In the early 1970s, many courts attempted to consider the notion that there was a constitutional theory of privacy that applied to criminal history records, and in particular to arrest records.

The courts prohibited the release of arrest records to the public where it could be shown that such release would result in some tangible stigma. By 1976, it can be argued from an analysis of the case law (see Belair 1988) that the prohibitions on public disclosure were there as a matter of legislative choice and constitutional precept. However, in 1976 this nascent doctrine was

100

extinguished. The Supreme Court published a landmark decision, which had the effect of 'deconstitutionalizing' the disclosure of arrest records. In *Paul v. Davis*, the Court ruled that such records do not relate to private conduct and thereby do not qualify for constitutional privacy protection. *Paul v Davis* involved the following facts. During the 1972 Christmas season police departments in Louisville, Kentucky circulated a flyer containing the photographs and names of individuals they characterized as 'active shoplifters'. The plaintiff, who was listed on the flyer, had been arrested some 18 months earlier for shoplifting and the charges were still pending but he had not been convicted. He sued, claiming among other things, invasion of privacy. In addressing the constitutional privacy claim, the Supreme Court said that the constitutional right of privacy protects certain kinds of personal conduct, usually related to procreation or marriage. The Court said that Davis' claim was unrelated to these types of privacy considerations and concluded that the US constitution does not require criminal justice agencies to keep confidential matters that are recorded in official records:

> "[Davis] claims constitutional protection against the disclosure of the fact of his arrest on a shoplifting charge. His claim is based, not upon any challenge to the State's ability to restrict his freedom of action in a sphere contended to be 'private', but instead on a claim that the State may not publicize a record of an official act such as an arrest. None of our substantive privacy decisions hold this or anything like this, and we decline to enlarge them in this manner".   (424 US 693 (1976): 713)

With few exceptions, court decisions throughout the late 1970s and into the 1980s relied on *Paul v. Davis*. In 1985, for example, a Third Circuit Court of Appeals panel upheld the constitutionality of a New Jersey statute requiring that solid waste licence applicants be fingerprinted and a criminal history record check be conducted. The court rejected the contention that criminal history records were private within the ambit of the constitutional right of privacy:

> "The disclosures most vociferously objected to are records of criminal charges. These matters are by definition public. While it may be that when conduct resulting in the convictions or charges was engaged in the person who engaged in it expected that such participation would remain secret, that expectation was never reinforced by the law".
> (780 F.2d 221, 234 3d Cir 1985)

However, the picture at the state level was somewhat different. In 1974 statutes in only 24 states addressed the disclosure of criminal history information (US Department of Justice 1988: 8). By 1984, statutes in 52 states addressed this issue. State legislatures had, after the adoption of the LEAA Regulations of 1976, opted to make criminal history records generally unavailable (SEARCH Group 1984). Also as Belair points out, to the extent that noncriminal justice agencies retained a limited right of access, a number of patterns were emerging in state legislation:

"1. here is a clear hierarchy of noncriminal justice requesters: at the top are national security agencies; in the middle are private employers, especially those involved in providing sensitive services, such as the care of children and the elderly; and at the bottom are the press and the general public.;

2. there is a clear distinction in state legislation between conviction information and nonconviction information; state agencies demonstrate some willingness to release the former and almost no willingness to release the latter;

3. there is a clear distinction between in-state and out-of-state noncriminal justice requesters, not so much in the law as in the way the state central criminal history repositories have interpreted and applied the law;

4. some state central repositories retain discretion about record dissemination – more discretion than some of us would have expected;

5. state legislation places very little emphasis on subject consent. Unlike other kinds of privacy schemes that involve personal information, very few states, only four or five, tie record access to subject consent".

(Belair ibid: 14)

The SEARCH Group (1984) survey revealed that statutes in 15 states permitted access to conviction-only information, or conviction information plus pending arrests, to noncriminal justice, governmental agencies for specified purposes, but prohibited access of any kind to private employers or to the public (Alaska, Arkansas, Arizona, California, Connecticut, Illinois, Kansas, Minnesota, New Hampshire, New Jersey, North Carolina, Oklahoma, Oregon, West Virginia and Wyoming). Statutes in 8 states permitted conviction information or conviction information plus pending arrests, to be given to private employers for specified employment background purposes (Delaware, District of Columbia, Georgia, Indiana, Kentucky, Maryland, South Carolina and Washington). Statutes in 10 states provided both conviction and nonconviction information to governmental, noncriminal justice agencies for a narrow range of purposes, and to private employers for a few exceptional purposes (Idaho, Iowa, Louisiana, Missouri, Montana, New York, Texas, Utah, Vermont and Virginia. Statutes in only 8 states permitted conviction-only information to be shared with the general public, but in many of these this access is subject to special restrictions (Idaho, Iowa, Louisiana, Massachusetts, Michigan,

Mississippi, Missouri and Montana). Finally, statutes in 5 states give the public access to both conviction and nonconviction information, but in most of these states this access is subject to special restrictions (Florida, Nebraska, Pennsylvania, Rhode Island and Wisconsin).

As was pointed out earlier, after the *Paul v. Davis* case, the disclosure of criminal history data was'deconstitutionalized'. Since then, undoubtedly the most significant legal development with respect to open records was the decision in April 1987, by the US Court of Appeals for the District of Columbia in *Reporters Committee for Freedom of the Press v. the US Department of Justice* (816 F.2d 730 (DC Cir.1987)).

Robert Schackne, a CBS reporter, and the Reporters Committee filed the lawsuit in 1979. They were seeking the criminal history records of the Medico brothers, a family from Rhode Island that allegedly had a long association with organized crime. It was argued that under the Federal Freedom of Information Act agencies had to make available, upon request, agency records. In refusing the request, the FBI cited two exemptions under the Act, one of them being the 1924 recordkeeping statute (see above). The FBI argued that this statute effectively prohibits the FBI's release of records to the public. The Court of Appeals disagreed. The FBI's second exemption claim, and the more important one, argued that the release of the criminal record would constitute an unwarranted invasion of privacy. The Court rejected that claim on the ground that the privacy interest was minimal because the very same information is already in the public domain: the criminal history record is merely a compilation of data from original records of entry, which are themselves public. The Court also found that the public interest in criminal history records is high.

In May 1987, the SEARCH Group and the states of California and New York filed a brief with the Court of Appeals in support of the FBI and the US Department of Justice, requesting that the District of Columbia Circuit rehear the case. The brief argues that the Court had misunderstood the nature of current state law. The Court focused on the law with respect to original records of entry instead of focusing on the law on criminal history records. It was argued in the brief that with the exception of Florida and Wisconsin - records are regarded as confidential. It was further argued that the status of entry records was irrelevant. Such records were public because of the need to prevent 'secret' justice. Entry records therefore had a definite but different purpose to criminal history records. In the end, the Court decided against a rehearing. However, on 22 March 1989, the US Supreme Court accepted these arguments on appeal, and brought case law back to a point more coterminous with the pragmatic caution emerging from the 1970s and 1980s state legislation.

Special access At this point, it is worth detailing some examples of legislative provisions for so-called 'special claims for access'. As pointed out earlier, only a few states have opted for an almost open records approach. The norm has been to give special classes of noncriminal justice requesters greater access for specified purposes. In particular, following a 1984 Federal statute making funding to social service agencies dependent on such access, statutes in many states have been amended to permit agencies involved in providing child care or other services to children to have access to criminal history record information for pre-employment, background checks.

California's law, for example, has changed to permit access to conviction record information for pre-employment screening for people who work or are otherwise involved in child care and community care programs (see Cal. Health and Safety Code 1522c, 1596.871, 1597.80 West Supp. (1988)).

In 1984, Illinois also expanded access to criminal history records for child care providers. As of 1988 Illinois now permits state regulated child care providers to obtain both conviction and nonconviction information about prospective employees. In addition, Illinois' new law gives private, volunteer organizations that provide services to children, such as Boy Scouts, YMCA, access to conviction and nonconviction information for background checks. Illinois has also expanded access to criminal history records for private detective agencies, organizations employing security guards, individuals holding liquor licences, and schools conducting checks for current or prospective employees (see Ill. Ann. Stat. ch.23, 2214.1-2230 ; ch.127, 55a (27); ch.38, 206-3.1(a) and (b); ch.122, 10-21.9; ch.127, 55a (25) (all Smith-Hurd Supp. 1987). Connecticut has passed legislation that makes conviction information available to the State's Human Services Department for checks on prospective licensees of family day care homes (see Conn. Gen. Stat. Ann. 54-142k West Supp.(1988)). Over the last few years, Georgia's legislature has also adopted legislation which authorizes the disclosure of nonconviction information to governmental, noncriminal justice agencies for background checks regarding teachers, individuals working in child care agencies and holding private detective licences (see Ga. Code Ann. 43-38-10; 49-5-60 -49-5-69; 49-5-70 -49-5-74 Cum. Supp (1987)).

Iowa has adopted legislation which permits agencies operating substance abuse treatment programs for juveniles to obtain criminal history record information about prospective employees (see Iowa Code Ann. 692.2(5) West Supp. (1987)). The state of Virginia has legislation which authorizes checks about adoptive or foster parents, about applicants for citizenship, and about individuals applying for employment in public service companies where the employment involves personal contact with the public (see Va. code 19.2-389 Cum. Supp. (1987)). As a final example, Washington State permits release of conviction data to volunteer organizations for background checks about individuals who provide education, training, treatment, supervision or recreational services to children under 16 years (see Wash.Legis. Serv. ch.486 West. Supp. (1987)).

However, it is at the Federal level where there has arguably been the most important development. On 4 December 1985 Congress adopted the Security Clearance Information Act (Pub. L. No.99-169, 99 Stat.1009). This Act opens virtually all criminal history record information to the Central Intelligence Agency (CIA), the Office of Personnel Management, the Department of Defense (DOD), and the FBI for background checks for security clearances and for placement of people in national security duties. Prior to the adoption of the Act, state laws had varied greatly with respect to federal noncriminal justice agency access to criminal history records. In some states, the security agencies received everything; in others, they received partial information, and in very few, they received virtually nothing. The Act is likely to have a profound impact upon the flow of records outside of the criminal justice system (see SEARCH Group 1979, which estimates that in the late 1970s federal agencies were conducting over a million checks annually).

Another federal development came in 1987, when the FBI proposed a change in its long-standing regulations on disclosure. The FBI provides criminal history record information to federally-chartered banks, parts of the security and commodities industry and state and local licencing officials, but it could only provide conviction information and so called open arrest information. The 1987 proposal involved providing all criminal history information.

Even though only enlarging slightly the remit, it nevertheless is one more indicator of an emerging trend to make information more available to the noncriminal justice sector. In the next section, we review some empirical evidence on disclosure.

Extent and growth of non-criminal justice use

Not surprisingly in view of all this legislative activity, state criminal record repositories and the FBI report substantial increases in the number of noncriminal justice access requests which they receive (US Department of Justice 1988: 29). A survey conducted by SEARCH Group of the operation of the 50 state central repositories found that workloads had increased significantly because of inquiries from noncriminal justice users (SEARCH Group 1987). Specifically, 38 states in the survey described the access to their criminal record data. The states reported that 25 million inquiries were made annually by criminal justice agencies. Of those 25 million inquiries, 87 per cent were done by computer terminal and 13 percent by mail or telephone. These percentages are important to an understanding of the impact on the state repositories of the increasing workload caused by noncriminal justice inquiries. This is because, these inquiries are only very rarely terminal based. A finger-print card usually needs to be submitted in response, and that response is generally by mail or in some written form. The relative distribution of requests based on the SEARCH Group survey is: 88 percent are criminal justice inquiries and 12 percent are noncriminal justice inquiries. However, the disproportionate effect on workload of noncriminal justice requests is well described by Leuba:

"The process that repositories 'generally' use when a noncriminal justice inquiry comes in is as follows. A search is made of the name index to see if the inquiry can be answered based on a name search. If they find an individual who appears to match the request, they pull the fingerprint card from the file and do a visual verification to make sure the fingerprint card under the name index is the same individual. At that point, if they have made a match, they will pull the record and comply with any inquiry requirement. If there is no match at that point, it indicates only that the name inquiry could not lead to an identification; there may be an alias in the name file or an alias on the fingerprint card. Next, a technical search is generally made of the fingerprint file, both in the subject classification file and in the master file. If a match is found at that point, then the same visual inspection takes place and the criminal record is retrieved. If no match is made at this point, only now can you prove, based on a fingerprint identification, that you do not have a criminal record for that individual in the file".   (Leuba 1988: 29)

The 1987 SEARCH survey report indicates that matches are made on only 5 to 8 per cent of such fingerprint card inspections.

When the states were asked for reasons for the increase in the number of inquiries which they received in 1985 (ranging from an annual increase of one per cent to 59 per cent) some 26 states gave as a reason new legislation giving access to criminal history records to noncriminal justice agencies. The US Department of Justice report highlights the concern felt about the increase in noncriminal justice traffic:

"The Director of Arizona's repository, for example, reported that 'Noncriminal justice use increases drastically every legislative year. During the last three or four years, we've had at least one or two new laws each year permitting additional governmental agencies to have access. We also have new executive orders - three or four every year – authorizing access to state agencies for licensing and employment purposes. They've become major consumers of our resources.'. Similarly, the repository Director in Minnesota reports that, 'We are right now servicing more noncriminal justice requests than criminal justice requests.'. Illinois' officials make the same point". (US Department of Justice 1988: 30)

The published experience of one state, Maryland, provides some indication of the nature of the expansion (see Leuba 1988). Leuba's review points out that Maryland's enabling statute of 1976 provides for the means for both in-state and out-of-state private employers to gain access to criminal history information. Certain criteria govern access: jobs that place people in positions of significant trust in the community; and jobs involving trust with a particular good, such as money or a very valuable commodity (or information). Leuba points out that over the period from 1976-1986, the noncriminal justice inquiry level remained relatively low and static, and then from the early 1980s began to rise slowly. The inquiry level in 1988 was running at 200 hundred checks per month under the state statute. Under the Security Clearance Information Act, the Maryland repository received some 6,000 requests per month in 1988. In 1983, a law was passed requiring career and volunteer firefighters to undergo checks. They receive around 30 inquiries per month. In 1986, the Child Care Worker Act was passed, mandating agencies that employ public or private teachers, social workers, foster parents, bus drivers, school nurses, parks and recreation personnel to run record checks. According to Leuba this resulted in a massive number of requests, around 1,500 per month.

Apart from the survey work of SEARCH Group and limited statements from state legislatures, little commissioned empirical evidence exists on the rate of growth of noncriminal justice use. By far the most comprehensive study was undertaken by the US Office of Technology Assessment (OTA) which published its report in 1982 (Office of Technology Assessment 1982). Of the 21.3 million annual disclosures in 1980, 27 per cent, or 5.8 million, were for purposes of noncriminal justice use. In the largest system, the FBI Identification Division, 54 per cent of the disclosures were for such use. Laudon (1986) points out that the role of the FBI in supplying information to federal, state, and local governments for the purpose of employment grew rapidly during and after World War II. At that time, private defence contractors were added to the list of users – "Since then, with the growth of the defense establishment, nuclear utility industries, and the financial industry, the number of private employers and public agencies granted access by executive order and congressional assent has grown rapidly." (Laudon ibid: 116).

The OTA study found that around 60 per cent of the federal agency noncriminal justice use of federal files is for employment purposes, the remaining 40 per cent involving mixed uses mostly for entitlement and immigration functions. States also use the federal file, and this use is predominantly to screen applicants for state and local licences, and employment. However, as Laudon (1986) indicates, these statistics conceal the variety and penetration of noncriminal justice use. On licencing alone, a US report notes:

> "a 1974 American Bar Association study estimated that seven million people are employed in licensed occupations. This study counted a total of 1,948 separate state licensing statutes, for an average of 39 per state...New York State, for example, in addition to its firearms licensing requirement, requires a conviction records check for applicants for the following positions: professional boxers, referees and judges; harness racing officials; private investigators and guards; users or transporters of explosives; male employees of manufacturers or wholesalers of alcoholic beverages; employers of migrant labourers; most employees or members of national securities exchanges; professional bondsmen; operators of employment agencies; longshoremen and related dock workers; employees of check cashing businesses; top employees in insurance companies; horse owners, trainers and jockeys; employees of liquor stores and certain employees of bars; and funeral directors".
>
> (US Department of Justice 1981: 50)

Laudon adds his own comment on this growing list:

> "In my case studies I found municipalities exceedingly unrestrained in the use of local statutes to check such groups as 'go-go' dancers (California), peanut and candy vendors (North Carolina), and septic tank and limberger cheese makers (New York)". (Laudon ibid: 117-8)

Gordon (1990) states that best estimates from the US Bureau of Census suggest that nearly 20 million governmental workers at all level in over 80,000 governmental units are subject to criminal history employment checks. In New York, Gordon illustrates the trend by pointing out that requests for checks for noncriminal justice use jumped from around 100,000 in 1979 to an estimate of 209,000 in 1984. Gordon continues by pointing out that California makes even greater use of checks for employment and licencing:

> "As of 1983, more than 3.7 million state records had been reviewed for employment purposes. Access has gone from public agencies to

youth-serving organizations to banks; as Fred Wynbrandt, a California Department of Justice official and former head of the NCIC Advisory Board, says, 'It just crept and crept'".   (Gordon ibid: 66)

Disclosure: implications and issues

An adequate understanding of the level and growth of noncriminal justice disclosure requires explanations. However, we have reserved such explanations to chapter 7, where we attempt to integrate such as is known about the factors related to growth of disclosure with the nature of the criminal record endeavour itself. In this concluding section, therefore, we restrict ourselves to a review and analysis of the important policy implications of disclosure, together with related issues of relevance to the UK and USA.

There is no escaping the fact that discussion on the implications of disclosure involves several competing values and factual claims. At the most general level, there is perhaps the belief shared in both the UK and USA that people should be given a second chance, an opportunity to move to a new community and start life anew regardless of past crimes, to rehabilitate themselves through work and reintegration into a community, and that the community has an obligation to accept such persons. On the other hand, there is an equally powerful belief that the community has the right to protect itself from individuals likely to commit a crime, that people must be held responsible for their past behaviour, and that organizations must be held responsible for the character of their employees. There are also more specific conceptions.

We examine some of these conceptions below, briefly analyzing the interests served by nondisclosure and pointing to wider issues.

Employment, rehabilitation and recidivism

It is clear from the description of trends in the previous section, that there is now relentless pressure to increase the number of employment and licencing arrangements for disclosure purposes both in the UK and USA. In the UK, for example, the recent addition in 1992 of checks on 'taxi-drivers' will extend police checks to some 85,000 new individuals, with a predicted annual rate of in excess of 80,000 'taxi-driver'checks (see *Hansard Lords* 24.6.91, col 436). The most recent figures from the Home Office indicate that vetting under the terms of the 1988 circular (No102) is running at 540,000 per annum. There are further calls in the UK from retailers associations, the private security industry (see South 1988 and Johnston 1992 for discussions on this, together with the earlier ACPO report *A Review of the Private Security Industry* 1988), private nannies (see *Day Care in the Home*, report of the Working Mothers Association 1992) and staff of private children's homes (Sone 1991), those seeking infertility treatment (see Douglas *et al* 1992) and as an example from the USA, the case of library appointments (Lincoln 1989).

To contextualize the case for and against the expansion of disclosure, it is worth noting by way of background what we know about the population 'at risk'– that is, the number of people with criminal records in the working population and the prevalence of offending. US Department of Labor demographic estimates suggest that of the 40 million persons with a record of arrest in the US, about 26 million are labour force participants. In the UK around 5 million people have a criminal record, amounting to over one-fifth of the working population (Apex Trust 1990). UK studies of prevalence of offending now have a substantial pedigree (see for example, Wadsworth 1979; Farrington 1981; Harvey and Pease 1988). Together with the UK Home Office criminal careers cohort research (Home Office 1985a; Shaw and Lobo 1989) and the Cambridge Study (Farrington 1989), we now have an interesting picture of the proportion of the population which at some time in their lives commits an indictable offence and thus establishes a record. Farrington (1981) calculated that as many as 43 per cent of males and 15 per cent of females in the UK would be convicted of an indictable offence sometime in their lives. Similarly, the Home Office, in one of the early papers on the cohort series concluded that: "The cumulative conviction rate for males born in 1953 was about 30 percent by the time they reached the age of 28...This result is not out of line with the deductions made by Farrington" (Home Office 1985: 7). More recently, it has been revealed that of the 1953 cohort some 33 per cent of the males had been convicted by the age of 31 – almost 9,000 of the original cohort of 26,200. The 1958 and 1963 cohorts have only been followed up to the ages of 26 and 21. Results here indicate male convictions of 31 per cent and 26 per cent respectively (Shaw and Lobo 1989). Comparative data from the USA confirms the reasonableness of these estimates. A comprehensive review of convictions prevalence concluded:

"The best available estimates suggest that 25-35 percent of urban males will be arrested for at least one index offence in their lives...".

(Visher and Roth 1986: 89)

Given this skeletal background on the population 'at risk' from disclosure, we begin with the question, would (does) nondisclosure promote rehabilitation? Perhaps the most readily accepted reason for preserving nondisclosure of an official record is that doing so results in a manifest and material benefit to society. With respect to criminal history records, the manifest and material benefit potentially advanced by nondisclosure is that offenders may be rehabilitated and reintegrated into society far more readily if they avoid the stigma and the tangible, adverse consequences which may arise if their criminal history records are widely available:

"Their [offenders'] social handicap is considerably aggravated by the stigma of a criminal record, requiring additional efforts from social agencies to support the arduous process of social reintegration".   (Rotman 1986: 1027)

Employment is one way to reintegrate the offender into society. There are, however, significant statutory impediments in the USA at both federal and state levels to employment of offenders. As study by Downing (1985) found that state and federal statutes bar or restrict offender employment in around 350 occupations employing around 10 million people.

However, even if it assumed that the public availability of conviction records enhances employment barriers, the policy implications of such a finding may be modest:

"It is now a matter of settled law that conviction record information should be available to virtually all federal employers and to state and local licensing boards for various types of employment and licensing eligibility determinations. The more relevant policy question is whether *nonconviction* [our emphasis] information should continue to be unavailable to the public because public availability will frustrate rehabilitation and reintegration by denying or limiting access to employment and other valued statuses".

(US Department of Justice 1988: 35)

The same 1988 US Department of Justice report argues that what little empirical evidence is available is mixed with respect to the question of whether and how private employers would use nonconviction information. It is argued that while older research, in particular, suggests that employers make efforts to obtain records (see Miller 1972 for example), more recent studies don't reflect this (see US Department of Justice 1987). The situation in the UK, however, does not reflect this pattern. The most recent research from a national survey of 600 employers suggesting that over 84 per cent ask applicants about previous convictions (House of Commons Employment Committee Second Report *Recruitment Practices* Session 1990-91: 19). However, an Apex Trust report suggests a mixed picture (see, Apex Trust 1991).

If there are doubts about the extent to which employers seek records in the USA, there is also, according to the US Department of Justice, uncertainty about what employers do with such records once obtained (see US Department of Justice 1988: 40-42). Again, it is suggested that more recent studies indicate a less harsh view of applicants with criminal history records. An Illinois study quoted in Downing (1985), for example, surveyed 375 businesses throughout the state. More than 50 per cent indicated that they would hire ex-offenders; however, offenders with a long period of incarceration or with records of multiple arrest were viewed least favourably. In addition, survey respondents indicated that for certain types of positions of trust or critical responsibility almost any type of record would be a bar. Laudon (1986), however, argues precisely the opposite. His review of the existing evidence states that "most of the research on how criminal records are actually used by employers suggests that any record – regardless of the offense – is sufficient for dismissal. It is simply naive to think that employers will weigh carefully the characteristics of the crime against the characteristics of the job." (Laudon ibid: 257).

In the UK, evidence suggests that there is an unwillingness among employers to adopt policies which enable people with a criminal record to be employed on merit. Estimates suggest that only 17 per cent of the public sector and 11 per cent of the private sector knowingly employ ex-offenders (see House of Commons Employment Committee ibid: 23). Breed (n.d.) makes a similar assessment.

The prime reason cited for keeping criminal records disclosure minimal is that of rehabilitation. In the UK, this is of course, enshrined in the increasingly fragile 1974 Rehabilitation of Offenders Act. Rehabilitation, as a penal ethic, emerged early in the 20th century as an alternative to the long-established punishment model. However, by the end of the 1970s, it has been argued that the vast bulk of research has called into question the rehabilitative ideal (see for example Allen 1981). The result in both the USA and UK has been a shift away to a more justice-based model of 'just desserts'. It has been argued that a great deal of statistical research documents recidivism, notably in the USA three studies by the US Bureau of Justice Statistics: *Returning to Prison* (1984), *Examining Recidivism* (1985), and *Recidivism of Young Parolees* (1987). The 1984 report showed that in 14 states examined, nearly a third of the prisoners released from prison re-offended within three years, and a quarter were back in two years or less. The 1985 study demonstrated that a very high percentage of individuals entering prison had a prior record of incarceration. The 1987 report found that 69 percent of a group of young parolees were rearrested for a serious offence within six years; 53 percent were convicted for new offences; and 49 percent were returned to prison. Similar data is available from the UK: offenders starting their criminal career at a young age were more likely to continue to further convictions, with one third of those first convicted at age 20 reconvicted within 10 years (Home Office 1985a). In summary, therefore, some argue that empirical evidence suggests that the release of criminal records

112

may not have a significant impact on rehabilitation and reintegration. Employers, it is argued, may not base employment decisions on records, but even if they did, it is further argued by some that it may not be of importance from a rehabilitation standpoint because recidivism rates suggest that rehabilitation is difficult to achieve regardless of an offender's employment prospects.

Those who recommend or tolerate the use of criminal records in the employment screening process have, it may be argued, good intentions: the hope is that offenders are not put in a position where they will be tempted to commit new crimes, endanger the public, or endanger the interests of their employers. The hope is that the chronically violent, antisocial, or untrustworthy individuals can be separated from the otherwise 'criminal types' and restricted from employment in 'sensitive' jobs. However, this and the foregoing debate, conflates rehabilitation and reformation. Rehabilitation implies the action of re-establishing a degraded person in a former standing with respect to rank and legal rights, and to attempt to ensure that those rights are maintained over time. The attempt to help the offender return to and remain as a full member of society, with the status and obligations which that membership confers, is rehabilitation. If offenders are not rehabilitated in this sense when formal punishment ends, then de facto punishment persists. Rehabilitation serves as a means to limit punishment to the extent pronounced. The relationship with reform is not simple (see McWilliams and Pease 1990). Rehabilitation does not imply that the person to be rehabilitated must also be reformed; rehabilitation neither precludes nor requires reform. Indeed, in thinking of rehabilitation as the restoration of rights and rank, we have to acknowledge that for many offenders, it would be the establishment of never-experienced rights and obligations with which one was dealing, not their restoration.

Before leaving this issue it is worth bearing considering two related matters. The first concerns the impact of criminal records on the distribution of the wide array of public and private services and benefits. Laudon (1986) notes that little is known about the affect of disclosure, but he points to some evidence. Many public housing agencies in the USA seek to establish the 'desirability' of applicants; an arrest or conviction record is a principle determinant, according to local officials (see Marchand 1980: 99). Retail credit companies commonly monitor police 'blotters', newspapers, and public court records and include this information in credit reports. As much as 73 per cent of retail credit reports may have this information (Laudon ibid: 120). These reports are used by life insurers, and other institutions.

States and local educational programmes also use 'desirability' criteria either as explicit conditions for granting an educational benefit or because of the 'good moral character' requirements of the programme.

In the UK, similar considerations exist explicitly in some areas. For example, criminal injuries compensation. As mentioned earlier in the chapter, under Home Office circular guidance, police make check the background of applicants seeking criminal injuries compensation. The Criminal Injuries Compensation Board, in considering an award, may take into account the 'conduct, character and way of life of the applicant'. An example from a recent Board report illustrates this:

> "The applicant, a man of twenty seven, was assaulted in a nightclub. He received bruising and cuts on his face of moderate severity...It was later established that he had a list of 49 offences dating back over a period of 14 years, all but four of which had resulted in convictions. The offences were mainly for theft and dishonesty, but there were less recent convictions for crimes of violence. The application was disallowed...with the following comment: ...The applicant's character and way of life, as shown by his criminal convictions, is such that it is inappropriate that an award of compensation should be made".   (Twenty-Fourth Report,
> Criminal Injuries Compensation Board, Cm 536 1988, HMSO)

The second area that needs to be considered in this context is that criminal records themselves are the product of a criminal justice system which itself can operate in a discriminatory manner. In the UK in relation to black people several commentators have begun to provide a theoretical understanding of this issue (see Gordon 1988 and Waters 1991), while others have provided empirical studies in relation to sentencing (see Hudson 1989). Crow (1987) provides a review in which he concludes:

> "The indications of work to date are that black people's experience of criminal justice in the UK is very different from that of white people. One consequence of this is that the number of black people in Prison...is disproportionately greater than their representation in the population as a whole".   (Crow ibid: 303)

Laudon (1986) quotes work from the early 1980s presenting a similar picture (see for example Blumstein 1984). He concludes:

> "... there are disagreements about the extent to which minorities receive treatment completely out of proportion to underlying differences in criminality. Nevertheless, most district attorneys, defense lawyers, and judges I interviewed expressed concern that a national record system would

tend to nationalize local patterns of discriminatory law enforcement behavior". (Laudon ibid: 230)

In the USA the Equal Employment Opportunity Commission has argued that the use of arrest data, in particular, by employers to make adverse employment decisions has a racially discriminatory impact. The courts have largely agreed with this, except in those instances where employers can show that their use of arrest data is job-related (see Genz 1980 for an interesting review and analysis of the implications for this of Title VII of the 1964 Civil Rights Act). Of course similar tendencies also exist in relation to the criminalization of homosexual behaviour (see Crane 1984). A case can be made, in our view, that the release of information from criminal records can act as a hidden stratifier of social and economic power.

Data quality

Issues of criminal record data quality were referred to in chapter 3. There is no doubt that such matters are highly pertinent to an analysis of the implications of disclosure.

There are four areas where release of record information could cast the person in a false or inaccurate light:

1.   the information relates to a different person;
2.   the information is inaccurate or incomplete;
3.   the information is accurate and complete but relates to a conviction or arrest that was improper;
4.   the information is accurate and complete but it relates to an 'old' record, no longer reflective of the subject's character.

In relation to identity matching, this is clearly a problem without fingerprint requirements. In respect of inaccuracies and incompleteness, the UK Home Affairs Committee *Criminal Records* found evidence of both (see chapter 3). In the USA disposition reporting remains the most serious problem of data quality, with reporting levels as low as 25 per cent in some states. Wilson (1988) notes:

"if the public were to have open access it would be faced with inaccurate or ambiguous data 40 percent of the time". (Wilson ibid: 21)

On improper conviction and arrest, federal statutes do not afford a definitive right to seal or purge records, however, the federal Civil Rights Act and the Privacy Act have been invoked successfully to obtain relief from improper records.

Finally, in relation to 'old' records, in the UK there is of course the 1974 Rehabilitation of Offenders Act – but this is riven with exceptions and exemptions. In the USA, statutes in at least seven states recognize that offenders with old records should necessarily have them disclosed. The Supreme Court has observed that after 20 years, a person is no longer a public figure merely by virtue of a conviction (Wilson ibid: 21).

Where to for disclosure?

As mentioned previously, issues of disclosure are complex and riven with conflicting values and purposes. In the UK, a recent Home Office report *The National Collection of Criminal Records* (Home Office 1991) has made a substantial number of recommendations about the future role and extent of disclosure. These new recommendations are dealt with, as part of a review of the that report, in the final chapter of this book. Here, we therefore reserve our conclusions to a summary of the latest standards on disclosure issued by SEARCH Group (SEARCH Group 1988), as they perhaps are the best guide to future trends in the USA.

SEARCH Group in the background to their updated standards, point out that they have revised the standard dealing with disclosure in the light of: increasing justifications for disclosure on national security grounds; new technology; research on rehabilitation; and the changing constitutional framework for confidentiality of records.

It is standard 13.5 that is significant. It reads:

"All criminal history record information in the possession or control of a criminal justice agency, except nonconviction information and criminal index information, shall be made available, upon request, to any person for any purpose, and nonconviction information and central index information shall be made available for governmental or private noncriminal justice purposes as authorized by state statute or court order or rule in circumstances involving responsibility for the life or safety of individuals. Nonconviction information and criminal index information may be made available under this standard only pursuant to a written agreement with the requester reasonably designed to ensure that the information is used for the purpose for which it was disseminated, is not redisseminated, and is maintained in a manner to assure the security of the information and the protection of the privacy interests of record subjects".

(SEARCH Group 1988: 26)

In comparison with its 1975 standard, SEARCH Group have recognized that they were 'swimming against the tide' of greater disclosure and have made amendments. The revised standard draws a sharp distinction between conviction and nonconviction information, but it is clear that all members of the public are entitled to access, for any purpose. However, in the commentary to the standard, SEARCH Group point out that it does not have the effect of making information available to the casual or curious requester. A preceding standard (10.1) only allows criminal justice information to be made available on the basis of positive identification by means of fingerprints. As a practical matter, this requirement means according to SEARCH Group that record subjects will have notice of such a request and will generally have given their approval in order for the requester to obtain their fingerprints.

Standard 13.5 permits access to nonconviction information for private noncriminal justice purposes in circumstances involving responsibility fro life or safety, and where authorized by state statute or court order or rule. This standard contemplates that some governmental licencing determinations, and some employment determinations, should properly be viewed by state legislatures and the courts as involving responsibilities for life or safety. Finally, the requirement that noncriminal justice requesters who obtain nonconviction information assure that the privacy interests of record subjects are protected means that some reasonable provision must be made for implementing data quality, subject access and the other privacy protection provided by the standards.

6 To minimise future risk: The politics of protection

Introduction

The disclosure of criminal records outside of the criminal justice system has seen a rapid growth over the last two decades with reference to child protection work. The abuse of children by those who care for them has increasingly been recognised as a 'problem' requiring a concerted social response from social workers, paediatricians, the police, health visitors, teachers and others concerned to ensure the protection of children. This formal response has conventionally been directed at parents and other adult carers within a given household. More recently has come a recognition that abuse of children can come from non-related adults in employment with children or in formalised caring positions such as child minders or foster-parents.

The disclosure of criminal records outside of the criminal justice system to enable the vetting of those seeking work and positions that will give them access to children in, say, childrens homes or schools, now takes place in a number of countries. Similar disclosures are made on those applying for 'caring positions' of trust with children but which are not regarded as paid employment positions. Such 'vetting' of people by reference to their criminal record provides a case study and gives us an insight into the nature of criminal record maintenance and its perceived usefulness outside of the criminal justice system, to decide on the suitability or otherwise of certain people to carry out certain tasks.

The rationale for vetting

It probably goes without saying that most societies expect those adults charged with the care of children as part of their work to carry out their task in a caring and sensitive manner. The relative dependence of the child on the adult requires a degree of trust in the caring relationship. When the child is particularly vulnerable due to earlier physical or sexual abuse, or is in some other way socially disadvantaged, the degree of trust required is arguably greater. Physically handicapped children or mentally impaired children are equally in need of well motivated care to ensure they develop to their full potential.

Particular regimes of residential child care and forms of education have, at times, come in for criticisms (see eg. Kahan and Levy 1991). Our concerns here, however, are with unacceptable and abusive behaviour from individuals given positions of trust with children in the workplace and elsewhere. Behaviour that usually comes to light following prosecution of the adults concerned (see eg. Mills 1989; McDonald 1990; Nelson 1992). On occasions the abuse is wide-ranging over a long period and involves more than one perpetrator, such as in Leicester in the UK (O'Sullivan and Jones 1991), California in the USA (Reed 1990), or the Kincora children homes 'scandal' in Belfast, Northern Ireland (Norton-Taylor 1989).

The incidence of abuse of this nature is not easy to record, but it is universally condemned as a breach of trust and an offence against common decencies. The social response has been to tighten up the selection procedures for posts giving access to children and to include a vetting arrangement that involves disclosure of any possible past convictions that might indicate someone is unsuitable to work with children. We will examine in some detail the vetting arrangements in England and Wales together with comparative arrangements in other parts of the world, and offer a critique of these arrangements.

England and Wales

A concern to protect children from adults with a criminal record can be traced back in England and Wales to the 1930s. The 1936 Public Health Act prevented anyone from becoming a foster-parent if they had:

> "been convicted of any offence under Part 1 of the Children and Young Persons Act 1933, or Part 2 of the Children Act 1908 or any offence of cruelty under the Prevention of Cruelty to Children Act 1904".
> (Public Health Act 1936 s.210 (c))

The 1936 Act s10(c) was subsequently repealed but it does represent an early concern that people with certain criminal records should not be allowed to have access to children as foster parents.

In the mid-1950s discussions took place between civil servants and the police on ways in which convictions could be released to ensure school teachers with certain criminal records did not gain access to children. It is clear from public records of the time that the Minister of Education "was being pressed to take more effective action to protect children from perverts". At this time, of course, prior to the 1967 Sexual Offences Act any sexual activity between male adults could result in a conviction, and there is evidence of particular fears being engendered by the "unfrocked cleric" (PRO HO 287/251 XC 186869)

The police were also anxious "that when acting on the strength of information given by the police, education authorities must not reveal the source of their information", and there should be no risk of libel actions against the police resulting from the assistance given. Such hopes to conceal sources could not be met for the police, and their concerns regarding libel still exist to the present day (PRO HO 287/251 XC 186869). The resulting Home Office guidance to Chief Constables advised on the need to disclose criminal convictions to the Ministry of Education when existing teachers were brought to court (Home Office 1954). The vetting of applicants to the profession was postponed to a later date.

In 1955 new arrangements to 'vet' foster parents by reference to criminal records were introduced. Local authority Childrens Departments were charged with ensuring that any applicant who had "been convicted of any offence which would render it undesirable that the child should associate with him" should not become a foster parent (Boarding Out Regulations S1 1955 No. 1377 para 17(1)(g)). Private foster parent arrangements were similarly subject to criminal record checks (see Foster Children Act 1980 s7(1)(c)).

Childminders providing day care for children had been regulated by health authorities since the 1948 Nurseries and Child minders Regulations Act. In the early days advice from the Ministry of Health was "that inquiries might usefully be made of the police" where this was indicated (Ministry of Health 1968: para 5(f)), and this was later formalised when local authorities had taken over the function (Home Office 1982: see also Dept. of Health 1991 (b)).

The Adoption Agencies Regulations 1959 Regulation 5 (e) made demands on local authorities and other adoption agencies assessing applicants to adopt to ensure "whether the authority have reason to believe that it would be detrimental to the infant to be kept by that person in those premises," and included a need to check criminal records. DHSS guidance was vague as to how access to the record would be made but advised that adoption agencies "should not disclose the source of their information" (DHSS 1977:42). The regulations were updated in 1983 and social services departments, now moving more centrally into adoption matters, given guidance to "make the usual inquiries of the police" (DHSS 1984: para 63; see also Hebenton and Thomas 1990). At the time of writing the Department of Health was coordinating an inter-departmental review of adoption procedures including arrangements covering the increased numbers of children being adopted from overseas.

In the wider field of protecting children in their own home the early seventies saw attention turned to the disclosure of criminal records. The watershed inquiry into the death of seven year old Maria Colwell in Brighton (DHSS 1974) led to a flurry of activity bordering on "moral panic" (see eg. Parton 1985) and the creation of a more formalised response to child abuse from health and social service agencies concerned. Central to this response was the perceived need to pool information to gather the complete 'picture' of what was going on in a given household. The case conference involving all the practitioners concerned sitting round the table became the manifest symbol of inter-agency cooperation, with the police being invited to take their part in the discussions.

The critical input made by the police was the disclosing of previous criminal convictions to the case conference, considered relevant: those "which are not relevant should not be revealed" (DHSS 1976: para 9). At times there have been disputes over what is and is not a relevant conviction (see eg. London Borough of Lambeth 1987: 147-153: London Borough of Islington 1989 para 12.5) but the presence of the police at what are now re-named child protection conferences has become a firmly established part of child protection procedures.

The late seventies also saw yet another new departure in the use of the criminal record in the interests of child protection. This was the new arrangements entered into to disclose the records of those who had been convicted of offences against children in the home at the point at which they were discharged from prison. The criminal record was passed from prison to probation service and social services departments covering the area the prisoner intended to live in when discharged. Social services departments were to check out the address given, with a view to ensuring the well-being of any children who might be living there (DHSS 1978). Again the system has not always worked smoothly (see eg. London Borough of Lambeth 1987: 152-3) and critics have argued that the arrangements should be widened to include those convicted of similar offences 'outside' the home and those who have received non-custodial sentences for similar offences (Kahan and Levy 1991: para 16.31; see also chapter 4).

In the mid-eighties attention had turned to the use of criminal records in the selection of employees who would have access to children. Until now the focus had only been on those positions of trust which included 'natural' parents, child minders, foster-parents and adoptive parents. Teachers in employment who committed offences would be reported to their employers, but vetting, as such, was not part of the initial selection process. The catalyst for change was the conviction in 1984 of Colin Evans for the murder of four-year old Marie Payne (Boseley 1984).

During Evans trial it came to light that he had carried out voluntary work with children for Berkshire Social Services Department, even though he had a string of previous convictions involving children. Although Evans had not met his victim through this work, a debate was entered into as to who should and should not have access to children in the course of their work. The Home Office and DHSS established a joint working party with the brief to "divise a system" to ensure that criminal records would, in future, be disclosed to those making decisions on the employment of local authority staff with access to children. The brief did not include a wider view on the nature of sexual offending or child abuse, nor did it require the working party to look at issues relating to the rehabilitation and employment of ex-offenders (Home Office/DHSS 1985b).

The resultant administrative guidance issued jointly by the Home Office, DHSS, DES and Welsh Office gave an outline of how local authorities should devise local systems with their local police forces on the exchange and processing of criminal records. The opportunity was also taken to consolidate all previous thinking on arrangements covering foster-parents, adoptive parents and child minding applicants (Home Office 1986 (b)). The Home Office sent further circular guidance to Chief Constables recommending the response the police should make to such requests from local authorities. Somewhat of a formality as the guidance had already been discussed in some detail with the Association of Chief Police Officers (ACPO) before the circular had been drafted (Home Office 1986 (a)).

Home Office Circular 86(44) (Home Office 1986(b)) introduced the concept of 'substantial access' to children as a guiding principle on the need to vet. Following selection of a new appointee, a criminal record check was to be requested. A list of possible posts was included containing social workers, childrens home staff, teachers, school groundsmen and others. Considerations to be taken into account included the degree of supervision available, the degree of one-to-one contact, the regularity of contact and whether or not the children could be described as 'particularly vulnerable'. Liaison with the police was through a single point – the 'senior nominated officer' – to assist in keeping information confidential.

Circular 86(44) allowed a good deal of discretion on its interpretation. Senior nominated officers receiving a criminal record could ratify or veto an appointment or they could refer the information back to the selection panel who had interviewed the applicant in the initial stage. A 'problematic' record was to be interpreted by reference to how long ago it was, what sentence had been imposed and how frequent the offending had been. The question of the relevance of the conviction was open to interpretation. Whilst offences against children might be uncontentious, other convictions were less clear cut. In Kent, for example, it later became known that the Director of Social Services had instructed staff that if in doubt "to 'err' on the side of caution by not employing anyone with 'any' record" (Brindle 1989 emphasis added). For their part the police were passing through the whole criminal record with no comment on what they considered relevant. This was in contrast to the input they were making to child protection conferences where they did make decisions on relevance.

The 1986 circular was also instrumental in introducing three other dimensions into vetting procedures. The first was to make changes to the Rehabilitation of Offenders Act 1974 which allowed people to ignore certain offences after a given period of time during which no further offences had been committed. The day after the circular was published, the Rehabilitation of Offenders Act 1974 (Exceptions) (Amendment) Order 1986 came into force allowing the police to disclose convictions formerly considered 'spent' under the 1974 Act, but to be disclosed when vetting those wanting to work with children.

Secondly the police's long standing fear of being sued for libel reared its head again. Authorities were asked to sign an indemnity against any liability incurred as a result of the police providing information under the new arrangements. Some authorities held out against giving any such indemnity and questioned why the police should be protected against maintaining inaccurate information (see eg. Hyder 1988). The present authors have queried elsewhere, why there was a need to change from the old system whereby the Home Office held indemnity for all police forces, to one requiring all local authorities in receipt of criminal records, to sign one (Thomas and Hebenton 1991b).

Finally the new arrangements led people to question what actually we mean by 'criminal records' being disclosed for vetting purposes. It became clear that the Home Office was quite happy for the police to disclose what it called 'other information' as well as straight criminal conviction records (Home Office 1986 (a): para 7). Such 'other information' could include acquittals or any other police intelligence held on a person. The nature of 'other information' is potentially as wide as the police wish to make it, and its interpretation by the receiving local authority can be problematic. From the applicants point of view it could include information that they were unaware the police held on them.

Within two years of the publication of Circular (86) 44 most local authorities had entered into arrangements with their local police forces and were vetting all applicants for work with 'substantial access' to children. The DES issued complementary guidance to independent schools offering to act as an intermediary if any of them wanted to check their staff (DES 1987) and the DHSS extended arrangements to NHS staff and volunteers offering "lengthy in-patient care" to children (DHSS 1988).

Initial complaints about the new system were focused on the inordinate length of time it seemed to take the police to respond to a request for a check. In some authorities a wait of 8 to 12 weeks was reported (Hyder 1988; Platt 1988). But the NCCL (now Liberty) began picking up complaints of a different nature, from individuals who felt they had been improperly excluded from employment by a police check. Examples were given of irrelevant and outdated offences being taken into account (NCCL 1988) and the weekly journal "Social Work Today" carried an anonymous article by someone refused work, entitled "Treated like a criminal – Ten Years On" (13 March 1988).

Further criticism came from the voluntary sector when it was suggested that criminal record checks be introduced into the selection of volunteers wanting to work with children (Mitchell 1989). Critics in the voluntary sector were far more vocal than the generally acquiescent local authorities statutory sector had been in 1986, when the introduction of checks had "raised hardly a ripple of public or professional debate" (Unell 1992: 18). In contrast voluntary sector workers found screening offensive (Rankin 1989) and expressed dismay "that there is not more concern about the procedure as a whole" (letter to *Social Work Today* 31 March 1988). A group of voluntary agencies established the Police Checks Monitoring Groups that published its own critique of the checks (PCMG 1988). A major concern was that volunteers would simply not be forthcoming if they felt they were going to be subject to a criminal record check (see also The Kenilworth Group 1989).

Possibly to placate the critics, the Home Office did not go straight into a system of police checks for the voluntary sector as it had done in the statutory sector. Instead it proposed a number of pilot schemes that would feel the way for the voluntary sector. The three schemes were to be in Dudley in the Midlands, Lancashire, and for the London based National Council of Voluntary Child Care Organisations (NCVCCO) which would offer a national scheme to participating organisations. Three options on disclosure were available to the three schemes. Option 1 followed the statutory sector by disclosing the complete record to the decision makers, Option 2 kept the disclosed record at a central 'disclosure unit' where decision makers could inspect it, and Option 3 provided for restricted disclosures of specified offences (Home Office 1989b).

An evaluation report on the pilot schemes produced a wealth of observations that had been conspicuous by its absence from the statutory sector arrangements. Approximately 3,500 checks were processed by the three pilot schemes in their first twelve months of operation. Eighty percent were processed by the national scheme, 15 per cent by the Lancashire Scheme and 4 per cent by the Dudley Scheme, with most checks using Option 1. 265 checks proved positive, or 7.4 per cent of the total.

Where records had been undisclosed by the applicant it was found most subjects had not deliberately concealed information but were unaware of the conditions of disclosure. Evidence also came to light of checks being superimposed on inadequate selection procedures, being run on volunteers not wanting to work with children and being run retrospectively on existing volunteers; this all contravened the guidance of the Home Office (Unell 1992).

On the 'relevance' of offences the evaluation study found evidence of non-relevant offences being taken into account on the basis that they might not directly impinge on the physical safety of the child but did indicate a lack of personal and moral example. As such volunteers seemed "largely unprotected from indiscriminate use of checks" with the Home Office Circular guidance (Home Office 1989) proving "irrelevant as a means of regulating demand for checks". Agencies were anxious to avoid any sort of risk, working to the 'what if' principle which resulted in "the safety of the child often appear(ing) to be confused with the safety of the organisation" (Unell 1992: 104-5). Future developments indicated a need for restriction to a range of given offences and a code of practice for child protection that agencies should adhere to (Unell 1992: 112).

During the summer of 1992, the Steering Committee with oversight of the pilot schemes closed down the Dudley and Lancashire schemes. The national scheme, operated through the NCVCCO, was allowed to continue for a further period and will also continue to approve new participants to the scheme. The overall aim was to target those child care positions thought particularly sensitive or difficult to supervise (Home Office letter ref. POL/92 1550/1/26 dated 24 August 1992).

As the pilot schemes for the voluntary sector were being put into place the Government issued a revised circular for the statutory sector in December 1988. Circular 102/88 (Home Office 1988b) was to update the 1986 circular (86) 44. The changes could not be described as major, and in many respects there were no changes at all. Minor revisions were made to the notion of "substantial opportunity for access" with some additional thoughts on the extent of supervision and the nature of "regular contact". Agency staff and private contractor staff were included in the checking arrangements, although a reminder of this fact had later to be sent following the conviction of an agency worker in a childrens home (SS1 1989). One idiosyncratic feature of this arrangement was the guidance that criminal record information should never be passed back to an employing contractor. If the employee chose not to say anything the contractor would have a staff member that he couldn't place in a local authority setting but not know why.

The new guidance gave ambiguous messages regarding the need to check students on work placements with access to children. It suggested that checks were not required unless information came to light suggesting otherwise (see Thomas 1989).

Further elaboration was given on the definition of 'other relevant information' besides straight criminal records. The Home Office stated that it would now include:

> "factual information which the police would be prepared to present as evidence in court, or details of acquittals or decisions not to prosecute where the circumstances of the case would give cause for concern."
>
> (Home Office 1988b: para 17 footnote)

Acquittals might be expected to include so-called technical acquittals, for example, where a childs evidence was found insufficient to secure a prosecution. Some acquittals clearly being less acquittals than other acquittals in some circumstances!

Home Office Circular (86) 44 as revised by Circular 102/88 continues to inform the essence of arrangements for vetting in the statutory sector. Neither have been the subject of debate in any democratic political forums (see eg. Hebenton and Thomas 1989), and both are only concerned with "devising a system" as the original working party brief that preceded them suggested. Critics have tried to set these systems in a wider context and to point out the erosion of the premise on which the 1974 Rehabilitation of Offenders Act is based, that, personality traits leading to certain behaviour, are not, for example, necessarily constant, and that situational factors can be as important in determining causes of crime (Thomas and Hebenton 1991b).

Others have taken the line that if we have to have vetting then it should at least be carried out in a clear and just manner. The National Association for the Care and Resettlement of Offenders produced guidance explaining how checks were carried out, how they linked in to the Rehabilitation of Offenders Act 1974, and what were the best tactics to adopt in confronting them as a job applicant (NACRO 1990). Other general guidance on the working of the 1974 Act was offered (Apex Trust 1989 and 1990) and the National Council for Civil Liberties argued for better staff training on the interpretation of criminal records, more rights to challenge for applicants, including a right of appeal, and for the Home Office to start some overall monitoring (NCCL 1990).

The Home Office entered into a consultation process in July 1992 aimed at updating Circular No. 102/1988 in the light of experience and also Unell's research (Unell 1992). Conscious of the "considerable strain on the police service" and with checks running at 5 times the level expected when the service was introduced in 1986, the Home Office was suggesting a two-tier system of vetting of 'ordinary' checks and 'sensitive' checks. These varied with the degree of supervision and vulnerability of the child which would determine which sort of check would be called for.

It was proposed that all posts should be subject to a PNC2 check on the criminal names and criminal conviction index and where necessary the NIB, but a 'sensitive' check would also require a search of local records based on addresses the person had lived at for the past five years. It was the local record check that was considered to slow the process down and be particularly onerous and by reducing this requirement it was hoped to speed the whole process up. Teachers and day nursery staff were to have an 'ordinary' check, for example, whilst foster parents, child minders, probation officers and childrens homes staff would still have the full check. Local authorities were also to be encouraged to tighten up the role of senior nominated officer to reaffirm the responsibilities of that job, and were also asked to help police by confirming a person's identity as far as they could (Draft Joint Circular 1992 Home Office letter of 9 July). A new request form for a check was also proposed (ibid: Annex D; see figure 10).

Consultation was being made until September 1992. Anomalies revealing themselves included an 'ordinary' check on education welfare officers but a full check on local authority social workers who might both be expected to have equal access to equally vulnerable children. The reduction of the local checks on non-reportable offences, bind-overs, cautions and other information would also be a short term phenomena if the long term computerization of the national criminal record system was eventually to include all of these categories of record on the PNC2 and to result in the closure of all local criminal record offices (see chapter 7). The new national checks on PNC2 and NIB would also continue to include 'other information' from the NIB microfiche where soft information is still held jointly with hard information. There is also no mention in the July draft circular of the Rehabilitation of Offenders Act being a part-determinant of disclosures as had been suggested by the Home Office Scrutiny Report (Home Office 1991: paras 145-150; see also chapter 7) and all 'spent' convictions were still to be disclosed whatever the status of the check.

The only monitoring of the vetting in the statutory system that had taken place had been coordinated by the Association of Metropolitan Authorities working with the Association of County Councils and the Association of District Councils. The survey carried out in January and February 1990 sought to indicate the success or otherwise of checking procedures, by recording the

Figure 10

```
                        (LOCAL AUTHORITY HEADING)

REQUEST FOR POLICE CHECK IN RESPECT OF APPLICATION FOR APPOINTMENT,
APPROVAL OR REGISTRATION INVOLVING SUBSTANTIAL ACCESS TO CHILDREN

A.  To be completed by applicant in BLOCK CAPITALS

I have made an application to the above-named local authority.

I understand that this work is subject to a police record check.  This has
been explained to me and I am aware that spent convictions may be
disclosed.  I hereby declare that the information I have given below is
true and I give my consent to a check being made.

(Signature)......................(Date)................................

Surname ...................      All Forenames .....................

Maiden Name ...............      Any previous surnames .............

Date of Birth ..../..../....  Place of Birth ....................Sex M/F

Present Address
..........................................................................

Previous addresses in last 5 years     Date from       and to:

..................................      ..............    ............

..................................      ..............    ............

..................................      ..............    ............

Have you ever been convicted at a court or cautioned by the police for any
offence?    YES/NO

If yes, provide details overleaf, including approximate date, the offence,
and the court or police force which dealt with you.
```

```
B. To be completed by the Senior Nominated Officer

Applicant to become
.........................................................

The person identified above satisfies the conditions for requesting a
police check set out in Joint Circular          .  The particulars
provided have been verified and I am satisfied they are accurate.
Please check (tick box):

national police records    [  ]    national and local police   [  ]
(for posts in nurseries,           records (for prospective
playgroups, day schools,           adoptive and foster parents,
youth and community work           childminders, posts in residential
etc)                               homes and boarding schools, social
                                   workers, probation officers etc)

.......................... (Signed) ................... (Date)

(* delete as applicable)
```

```
C. For Police Use Only.                      Ref: _____

PNC *and other records have been checked against the above details:
(* delete as applicable)
             [  ]    No trace on              [  ]    The subject appears
                     details supplied                 identical with the
                                                      person whose criminal
                                                      record is attached

..........................(Signed) ................... (Date)
```

ALL FORMS TO BE RETURNED UNDER "CONFIDENTIAL" COVER

FEW-599-JAII

number of instances in which a potential employee was found to be unsuitable for filling a certain post. Results showed a considerable degree of consistency in practice with authorities stating that each case was treated on its individual merits. Failure to disclose could be taken as grounds for non-appointment and there was variation in decisions concerning cases not directly related to children, such as offences relating to drugs. A number of authorities were found to be vetting applicants for posts unrelated to children (AMA 1990).

At a higher political level criticism was also directed at the administration of vetting by the House of Commons Home Affairs Committee. Their report in April 1990 drew attention to the laissez-faire manner in which vetting had developed across the whole of the UK:

"The fact that 51 police forces might permit access (to criminal records) in a haphazard and unaccountable manner has worrying implications for the liberty of the individual. We believe that if the public were made aware of these arrangements, there would be an outcry".

(House of Commons 1990a: para 21)

The committee were concerned at the lack of accountability, the question of who was receiving the records, what information was being given and how we could be sure it was accurate.

The Government responded by commissioning an "efficiency scrutiny" from the Home Office, looking at all aspects of the maintenance and use of our national criminal record collection. The Scrutiny Report made a number of suggestions on the need to rationalise the fragmentary system they found and put its faith in computerisation to ensure accuracy and completeness of records. On vetting, it was still concerned that "substantial access" to children was being too loosely defined, was unhappy about the informal exchange of police intelligence by low ranking officers using the telephone, and recommended the institution of a new agency to hold records and a Vetting Agency to take this role away from the police. The Report saw no reason to split intelligence from other information held by the police, and that "after computerisation, vetting should be made more widely available to protect children", but with new safeguards on civil liberties built in (Home Office 1991)

The Governments response to the Scrutiny Report was to "acknowledge the weaknesses, which the report identifies, in the present arrangements for disclosing information from the criminal record for the purpose of assisting employers, licensing authorities etc. "and its intention to publish a consultation paper in Autumn 1992 outlining proposals for new disclosure arrangements (Hansard 1991 cols 533-4 22 Oct), (see chapter 7).

In fact most comment on vetting arrangements were far from critical and many called for their extension to other workers with vulnerable adult groups. The Home Office Scrutiny Report had suggested extending vetting to elderly, mentally and physically handicapped people (Home Office 1991: para 151) and indeed the checking of proprietors and officers in charge of residential care homes for elderly people had started 1st April 1991 (Dept. of Health 1991 (c)).

As far as children were concerned, a number of well-publicised child abuse cases effectively stifled any discussion of liberalising policy. An editorial in "Social Work Today" argued for an extension of the 'substantial access' idea to cover the normally desk-bound Directors of Social Services following the conviction for sexual offences against children of a Yorkshire Director who undertook voluntary work in his spare time ("Failure of one reflects on us all" *Social Work Today* 14 Sept. 1989). After the conviction of the officer in charge of a childrens home in Leicester for abusing children in his care over a number of years, the Government appointed a committee of inquiry into the recruitment and selection of staff to childrens homes. The committee was chaired by the former Director of Social Services for Kent Norman Warner, who in 1989 had taken a hard line in questions of "relevant offences" to be considered in employment procedures (see Ogden 1992).

The Committee of inquiry into the "Pindown" scandal of abusive procedures in Staffordshire Childrens Homes had also turned its attention to criminal record checks. The inquiry team recommended their extension to visitors to childrens homes and to landlords offering accommodation to young people leaving local authority care (Kahan and Levy 1991 chaps 15 and 16). The checking of nannies and aupairs working in peoples homes was advocated after the conviction of a nanny for assaulting children in her care (Oulton and Naylor 1992) and was further called for by a later more extensive report into the provision of day care in the home (Marks and Whitfield 1992; Working Mothers Association 1992).

Another attempt to introduce vetting in relation to children came from an unexpected quarter and concerned children not yet born. The development of new medical technologies to assist infertile couples and others to conceive had proceeded apace during the 1970s. The Government saw a need to properly regulate these new treatment centres offering in-vitro fertilisation, artificial insemination and other techniques. The Warnock Committee was asked to look at the issues raised (DHSS 1984) and after further consultation the Human Fertilisation and Embryology Act reached the statute books in 1990.

One of the more contentious aspects of the debate had concerned the right of non-married couples and single women to receive treatment. The Human Fertilisation and Embryology Act 1990 ruled that they could, but only after account had been taken to ensure "the welfare of any child who may be born as a result of the treatment (including the need of that child for a father)" (HFEA

1990 s13(5)). All treatment centres were to be licensed and a condition of receiving a license was, amongst other things, that arrangements should be in place to ensure the carrying out of Section 13(5). Comparisons were made with would-be adoptive parents or foster parents. The question then arose as to just what these arrangements were to be.

The 1990 Act had established the Human Fertilisation and Embryology Authority to give guidance on all matters relating to the Act, and in particular to produce a Code of Practice. A draft code of practice was published in 1991 for consultation together with an accompanying "Explanation" document (HFEA 1991 (a), HFEA 1991 (b)). It was clear that the Authority expected treatment centres to ensure the welfare of the unborn child by reference to information gathered from social services departments, G.P's and on the suitability of the applicant for treatment. The "Explanation" document expressed the need for discussions between the Authority and the Association of Chief Police Officers in order to arrange disclosure of criminal records (HFEA 1991 (b) para 3.18).

The final version of the Code of Practice (HFEA 1991 (c)), however, back-tracked on the explicit disclosure of criminal records to treatment centres and only referred in oblique terms to the need to "make such further inquiries of any relevant individual, authority or agency as it can" (HFEA 1991 (c): para 3.21). It would appear from discussions between the authors and the HFEA that there has been no formal agreement with the Home Office or the Association of Chief Police Officers to allow this particular proposed extension of vetting (for further discussion see Douglas et al 1992).

At the same time as these discussions on eligibility for infertility treatment were taking place the Government completed a major review of child care law with the Children Act 1989 which was implemented in October 1991. The 1989 Act revised the law on child protection and local authority care but made no direct reference to vetting as such. Supplementary guidance to the Act from the Department of Health, reminded local authorities to carry out police checks on staff in childrens homes (Dept, of Health 1991 (d): para 1.34) and on applicants to become foster-parents (Dept. of Health 1991 (e): para 3.17). The 1989 Act also included for the first time the welfare of children in small private boarding schools and again reminders of the need to check previous criminal convictions through the medium of the DES were made (Dept. of Health (f): paras 3.3.1 - 3.5.7 and Dept. of Health 1991 (g): paras 6.12 - 6.13).

Further guidance was given on the continuing availability of the Departments of Health's own Consultancy Service and the Department of Education and Science's 'List 99'. Both of these services provide information to local authority employers or people whose fitness to care for or work with children was in doubt. Both services are voluntary additions to criminal record checks and although the police may have provided some information to them, much of the information also falls short of having been 'processed' by the criminal justice system. At the end of 1989 the Department of Health's Consultancy Service held some 6,000 names on its register, with the person concerned being advised in writing and given an opportunity to appeal (see Hansard 20 Oct 1989 PQ's 4982-85; see also Home Office 1988b: Annex A).

An unexpected addition to the Children Act 1989 was guidance produced by the Department of Health concerning the vetting of child minders, private day care workers and private foster parents. With no prior discussion the Department of Health produced new regulations that directly confronted the question of what was or was not, a "relevant" offence to be taken into account when considering a criminal conviction record that might disqualify an already approved person. A Schedule appended to the Regulations listed those offences which would in future disqualify applicants to these posts throughout the UK (The Disqualification for Caring for Children Regulations S.1 1991 No 2094).

The offences included those specified in Schedule 1 of the Children and Young Persons Act 1933 concerning harm or injury to children and other related offences against children, together with offences involving injury or threat of injury to another person. Discretion to include other offences such as drug misuse, burglary or theft appeared to have gone. The Department of Health's published list was all the more noteworthy by appearing in the same month (October 1991) as a Home Office statement on criminal record vetting saying that 'positive' and 'negative' lists of offences was not "a safe or practical approach" (Home Office 1991: paras 146-7).

As these new regulations apply also to people approved to work in private registered childrens homes and voluntary homes as well as private foster parents, child minders or providers of day care (see Hansard 5.2.92 PQ 1201-4), there have been suggestions that vetting, at least as far as disqualification goes, has become regulated by statutory instruments in the private and voluntary sector and is still open to more discretionary administrative direction in the public sector. The Secretary of State for Health has denied any such intention and feels that equivalent measures exist in all sectors to ensure the welfare of children (Hansard 21.2.92 PQ 1435).

Scotland and Northern Ireland

The arrangements for vetting those wishing access to children in Scotland and Northern Ireland bear considerable resemblance to arrangements in England and Wales. We consider first the arrangements in Northern Ireland before moving to those that exist in Scotland.

Perhaps prompted by the allegations of long standing abuse in the Kincora childrens home in Belfast (see Lynch 1986), the Department of Health and Social Services in Northern Ireland established a Pre-Employment Consultancy Service in 1983. The Departments Child Care Branch offered the Consultancy Service to employers in the statutory and voluntary sector, acting as an intermediary between the employers and the police. On request from employers the Child Care Branch in turn requested criminal record disclosure from the Royal Ulster Constabulary and acted as a screening agency before passing on relevant offences only, back to the employer. The Child Care Branch could also add other information to the criminal record if they held anything, in much the same way as the mainland Department of Health Consultancy Service does for local authorities in England and Wales (DHSS (N1) 1989).

In 1989 this arrangement was altered following the recommendations of an Inter-Departmental Working Party and the Child Care Branch stopped acting as a screening agent for criminal records, and allowed statutory employers to have direct access to the RUC to receive a full criminal record history on those wishing to work not only with children but also mentally handicapped adults (DHSS (NI) 1989). The Child Care Branch continued to offer a Consultancy Service based on other information it might hold to the statutory sector and continued its former screening role with the voluntary sector. The Department of Education in Northern Ireland started vetting teachers and other school employees in similar fashion and were given direct access to police held criminal records. This was the first time teachers had been vetted in any form in Northern Ireland (DENI 1990). The RUC holds its own criminal record system with access to the London based Police National Computer via Merseyside police as required. In 1991 plans were in hand to give direct access to the PNC and to integrate Northern Irelands criminal records into the England and Wales national system (Home Office 1991: para 30).

The vetting of applicants to become foster-parents, adoptive parents or child-minders has always been carried out by direct contact between Health and Social Services Board social workers and the police, "under long standing" arrangements. These arrangements at one time permitted the police to convey "any information revealed by the check ... by telephone to the social worker who made the request". Such informal arrangements were replaced in 1989 by the introduction of written requests (DHSS (NI) 1989: para 25).

In Scotland arrangements for vetting are based on the original Home Office/DHSS Working Party of 1985 (Home Office/DHSS 1985b). Unlike the English and Welsh, however, who produced guidance for local authorities the following year in 1986, the Scots appeared much more willing to take their time in considering their response which appeared in 1989 (Scottish Education Dept. 1989). The lack of haste may have been attributed to the fact that some arrangements already existed before 1985 to check prospective employees in residential establishments for children and List D schools (SWSG 1985). The 1989 response sought to consolidate and rationalise these arrangements and bears remarkable similarity to the English version, maintaining the strictly procedural approach and with no reference to rehabilitation or the nature of offending against children.

The Scottish Circular does give more prominence than the English version to the need to place vetting systems in the context of well defined selection policies and practice. Neither the 1986 or 1988 version of the Circular in England and Wales state anything so clearly as that "checks should not form part of the selection process. They should be used to provide a final verification on successful candidates" (Scottish Education Dept. 1989: para 3).

On the question of "substantial access" on both sides of the border Circulars are agreed that close supervision should obviate the need for checking. The 1989 Scottish Circular, however, adds the rider that "the scope for developing relationships which could be exploited outside of working hours should be kept in mind" (Scottish Education Dept. 1989: para 11). This rider was present in the 1986 English version of the circular but was dropped from the 1988 version. Its re-instatement by the Scots may have been attributable to the publicity surrounding just such an exploitative relationship and a conviction taking place in England in November 1988 (Calderdale MBC 1989).

More substantial disagreement takes place between the English and the Scots over the viability of checking private contractors working on local authority premises. In England it is believed we should vet such contractors, whilst in Scotland it is considered "not practicable" (Scottish Education Dept. 1989: para 12).

Since October 1991 Scotland has been subject to the same regulations as in England and Wales concerning child minders, private foster parents and others, and as we have already seen, they now have a clear list of offences that can be taken into account (The Disqualifications for Caring for Children Regulations S1 1991 No.2094). In general the Children Act 1989 is not otherwise applicable in Scotland where a major review of child care law was being completed in 1992.

The Scottish Criminal Record Office based in Glasgow providing a single point of reference and therefore an efficient service to all Scottish police forces, has caused the Home Office to comment on "the considerable success of the Scottish system" (Home Office 1991: para 27). The turn-around time for vetting was, in particular, much faster than from the fragmented system in England. For the long term, however, the Home Office recommended an interface between the two systems, which did not exist in 1991, and ultimately the absorption of Scotlands 10 million or so records into a London based

National Criminal Record System alongside the records from Northern Ireland (Home Office 1991: para 28).

Europe

A variety of systems exist in Europe – including no systems at all in some countries – for assessing people's suitability to work or hold posts having close access to children. Interest in the different systems has grown amongst member states of the European Community as 1992 approached bringing with it the implementation of the Single European Market. With a potentially more mobile labour force the practicalities of how people were to be 'checked' out has had to move on to the question of how we will take account of different judicial systems if one country were to check them out against anothers different social and judicial background and even the more philosophical question of why checks should be carried out at all.

In England the Association of Directors of Social Services raised the question of whether people coming to the UK from Europe could have their criminal records checked and called for the "synchronisation of information requirements" with Europe and better "communication and links with employers and police forces" (ADSS 1992). A House of Commons Select Committee on employment recruitment practices was concerned that overseas workers were treated in no less favourable a way then people in this country when it came to employment vetting (House of Commons 1991). Questions put directly to the Commission of the European Communities asking what action was being taken concerning vetting and child protection, received only a brief and negative reply (*Official Jnl. of the European Communities* 21 May 1990 Written Questions No.'s 1244/89 and 1245/89).

Information collated by the UK Home Office in conjunction with the Foreign and Commonwealth Office has given us a picture of the extent and nature of vetting in EC member states (Home Office 1991 Annex Q). A number of countries use the issuing of 'good conduct' or 'good standard' certificates by authorities to applicants for work with children. This device avoids the use of direct disclosure mechanisms to potential employers and is the favoured method in Belgium, Germany, Holland and Spain. The Germans also point out that not only is it not possible for them to check the background of one particular group of persons, but that also there is no demand for it. Good conduct certificates have been criticised in the past by the Council of Europe looking at them on a Europe - wide basis because of the disparity of information held on them. Some were objective criminal records, others far more subjective offering potentially prejudicial comments on character and demeanour

(Council of Europe 1984: 35).

Denmark has arrangements to disclose criminal records to employers that bear some resemblance to the UK system, and similarly France allows disclosure but only in the vetting of officers in charge of establishments working with children. The Republic of Ireland makes no concessions for vetting job applicants but does allow disclosure of records to be made by the Garda regarding would-be foster parents or adoptive parents.

Portugal, Luxembourg, Italy and Greece require applicants to produce their own criminal record obtained from the relevant authorities, to show to employers. In Luxembourg only a record of imprisonable offences can be produced, known as the 'Extrait due Casier Judicaire', but this is considered sufficient in that offences against children would have almost certainly lead to imprisonment. This system of data subjects, requesting access to their own records for purposes of employment vetting has not been universally accepted. In the UK the Data Protection Registrar has specifically come down against this use of data subject provisions in relevant data protection legislation. Organisations in the UK have been asked to "consider very carefully both the propriety and the value of adopting a policy of attempting to vet applicants in this way" (Data Protection Registrar 1989). The European Parliament has also stated its belief that the practice should be discontinued throughout the European Community and amendments be made to the 1990 Draft European Directive on Data Protection to make it an offence for employers to make such requests of employment applicants.

Outside of the European Community Austria has stated that it does not carry out checks of criminal background with regard to employment. Norway and Sweden do carry out checks in much the same way as the United Kingdom with requests being accompanied by the subject's authorization (DENI 1990: Addendum).

United States of America

A number of well publicised incidents concerning abuse of children in the work place have occurred in the USA. The most notorious concerned the alleged molesting of children at a nursery school founded by Virginia McMartin in the prosperous suburb of Manhattan Beach in California. The mother of a two year old attending the school first reported her concerns to the police in August 1983, and set in train proceedings that lasted for the remainder of the decade. At one point it was alleged that up to 369 children had been sexually assaulted (Reed 1990). A wave of hysteria was also described as sweeping through the local community as accusations were fired in all directions leading to the closure of seven infant schools in Manhattan Beach and the suspicions that as many as 1,200 child victims could have been involved (Cockburn 1990).

The accusations were not confined to California, and the mid-eighties saw a succession of similar 'moral panics' breaking out "in more than 100 cities from Fort Bragg, California to Grenada, Mississippi" (Cockburn 1990) as allegations spread through the press, prosecutors, parents, social service workers and consultants. Comparisons were made with the 17th century Salem witch hunts in Massachusetts (see eg. Botsford 1990).

Whatever the truth behind this publicity, the United States has, as we have seen, (chapter 5), developed arrangements for the checking of criminal records over a number of years and in various forms. Initiatives at both federal and state level have led to a multiplicity of systems. Common to all of them is the underlying concept of a closed system of criminal records that can be disclosed outside of the criminal justice system in terms of a strict hierarchy:

> "at the top are national security agencies: in the middle are private employers, especially those involved in providing sensitive services such as care of children and the elderly: and at the bottom are the press and general public".   (Belair 1988:14)

Attempts had been made in the early 1970s to amend the law concerning the confidentiality of criminal records, When these attempts proved unsuccessful, the Law Enforcements Assistance Administration issued new Regulations in 1976 to tighten up on the accuracy and completeness of criminal records, as well as the degree of dissemination. The SEARCH organisation established in 1968 by the separate US States to advise on criminal information systems issued its Code of Practice in 1975 and has subsequently kept it updated (SEARCH 1988). By 1982 an estimated 350 occupations were subject of criminal record check (Wilson 1988: 18).

On the East Coast, Massachusetts had passed its Criminal Offender Record Information legislation, known as CORI, in 1972. Originally disclosures did not cover access to children employment, but amendments to the Act were made in 1977 following the conviction of a school bus driver for offences against children with whom he had contact in his employment. During the trial it came to light that the defendant had a history of convictions for sexual offences (Adelman 1990: 21).

Despite the growth of disclosures of records for vetting purposes, the particular vetting of those with access to children was sill considered by some people to be insufficient. Citing the Manhattan Beach allegations one observer decried the fact that "we have done virtually nothing to obtain the criminal history of those who are entrusted with our children", and what was required was:

> "legislation (which) would authorise public and private employer access to sexual criminal history records of volunteers of paid workers in child-related fields"   (Herrington 1986: 8)

In 1984 Congress had passed federal legislation that had tried to encourage individual States to introduce criminal record checks into employment selection decisions where child care was involved. The legislation did this by tying eligibility for about $25 million in social service block grants to the appropriate changes in State law. Alabama, Connecticut, Georgia, Minnesota and Iowa were amongst the first to change their laws to take up the incentive (Belair 1988: 16). In 1986 Maryland, for example, passed its Child Care Worker Act that mandated both private and public agencies that employed "school teachers, social workers, foster parents, day care centre workers, school bus drivers, juvenile services employees, school nurses, parks and recreational personnel ... and a number of others to run record checks" (Leuba 1988: 30).

The variety of systems in the different US States makes it hard to generalise about the operation of systems. In Massachusetts, for example, agreements on disclosure are made by a Criminal History System Board in discussions with a Security and Privy Council acting in tension with each other as a form of checks and balances. The only common standards for criminal record maintenance and for checks are the non-statutory ones published by SEARCH (see figure 11 for an example of a state's criminal record request form).

SEARCH offers a series of standards of which No. 13 concerns good practice in the "Dissemination of Criminal Justice Information to Noncriminal Justice Requestors". Sub-section 13.5 advises that disclosure for vetting those with access to children should only occur "as authorised by state statute or court order" involving the life or safety of individuals, and should not include non-conviction information such as intelligence, unless there is a written agreement with conditions of confidentiality attached (SEARCH 1988: 26).

Conclusions

The disclosure of criminal conviction records outside of the criminal justice system for purposes of vetting those with access to children provides a case study in the use of personal information to make judgements on the suitability of people for certain positions and roles. We have seen that disclosures of this nature are becoming widespread around the world and can cite further evidence, for example, that Saudi Arabia, Pakistan and Trinidad also carry out checks to protect children (see DENI 1990 Addendum). It is also clear that such vetting raises a number of questions at the operational level, but we believe that

Figure 11

Washington State Patrol

Identification and Criminal History Section
P.O. Box 2527, Olympia, WA 98507-2527

REQUEST FOR CRIMINAL HISTORY INFORMATION
CHILD/ADULT ABUSE INFORMATION ACT
Chapter 486, Laws of 1987
(Instructions on Reverse Side)

Ⓐ REQUESTOR'S AGENCY/ADDRESS

Agency
Attn.
Address
City State Zip

I certify that this request is made pursuant to and for the purpose indicated.

Authorized Signature   Date

Title

Ⓑ PURPOSE

☐ ESD/School District - no fee
☐ Non-Profit Busn./Org. - no fee
☐ Profit Business/Org. - $10
☐ Superintendent of Public Instr. Certification - $10

Fees:

Make payable to **Washington State Patrol** by cashier's check, money order, or commercial business account.

NO PERSONAL CHECKS ACCEPTED

Ⓒ APPLICANT OF INQUIRY

Applicant's Name: _____ Last _____ First _____ Middle
Alias/Maiden Name: _____
Date of Birth: _____ Month/Day/Year _____ Sex: _____ Race: _____
Social Security Number: _____ Drivers Lic. Number/State: _____ / _____

Secondary dissemination of this criminal history record information response is prohibited unless in compliance with RCW 10.97.050.

Ⓓ IDENTIFICATION DECLARING NO EVIDENCE
WASHINGTON STATE PATROL IDENTIFICATION & CRIMINAL HISTORY SECTION
As of this date, the applicant named below shows no evidence pursuant to Chapter 486, Laws of 1987.

WSP Use Only

Business/Organization Requesting Information

Applicant's Signature

Right Thumb Print (Optional)

Applicant's Name

Address

City State Zip

WSP-ID-430

questions should also be raised at a wider level of social theory.

We have focused, in particular, on the practice of police checks in the UK, but would contend that many of the operational issues rased there will be common to other forms of vetting. The arrangements entered into between criminal record repositories and the agencies entrusted with the disclosure information are notable for their 'low visibility' and for the lack of formal public debate that has been made on them. The nature of the 'public interest' in terms of making decisions based on disclosed records, is also marked by a public discussion that tends toward a 'common sense' approach.

It has always been held that criminal record repositories hold their records in a high degree of confidentiality. The increasing amount of disclosures for child care vetting and other purposes strains that confidentiality in two ways. The amount of disclosed information may be made to agencies who do not accord it the same degree of confidentiality, and the very act of making ever more disclosures will, arguably, weaken the need for confidentiality at the original repositories, and contribute to the growth of a new occupational culture that sees disclosure as being right and proper in almost any circumstances.

In the UK examples have emerged in the voluntary sector of agency staff simply "popping into the local police station with a list of names" on which they want a check run (Whitcher and Jones 1989). Other studies have revealed "less than leak proof practices" that included the handling of criminal records along with the "normal" post (Unell 1992: 92). In the statutory sector the Home Office uncovered:

"a well established unofficial practice – and all the more dangerous for that – for more junior (police) officers to read over extracts of intelligence files to trusted contacts in the relevant local authority departments".

(Home Office 1991: para 155)

Local authorities have also used 'trusted contacts' to check out those who would not normally have access to children by "informally check(ing) out prospective directors through their police networks" (Fry 1989). They have also deceived the police to check workers with adults "by keeping a single list of carers for adults and children and getting the lot vetted" (Rickford 1991) and to get voluntary agencies access to records by disguising their requests as their own (Unell 1992: 90). Needless to say such practices fall outside of the 'official' guidance from the Home Office even though they may be carried out with the worthiest of motives by the people concerned. It is these worthy motives that lie behind many of these "improper" actions, because child protection is given such an overriding priority by all concerned, and the couching of arrangements in administrative notes of guidance rather than substantive law must signal that there is a lesser sanction in ignoring them.

Such a cautious underlying approach toward vetting has been summed up by one senior officer in an English local authority:

> "We are not prepared to forfeit our client's safety, lives, sanity or childhood by taking just a small risk. Frankly, that isn't our business and not one we would want to be in".   (Cosgrove 1989)

In contrast there are now voices being raised that vetting by criminal record checks does not give value for money when it comes to protecting children. When some potential abusers will have no record anyway, checks become "an extremely inefficient and costly way to identify a very small number of other potential abusers". (Finkelor et al 1988: 67). In terms of resources taken up in carrying out criminal record checks the amount of 'hits' or disclosures revealing potential offenders can be out of proportion to the costs involved. In the UK, the Department of Health has signalled its concern:

> "Access by care agencies to police information on criminal convictions is a difficult matter which raises issues of cost, organisation and priorities, as well as civil rights".   (Dep. of Health 1991 (h): para 3.21)

In the USA the number of "hits" in one study has been put at 8 per cent of all checks (Finkelor et al 1988: 65-7) and in the UK at 7.4 per cent (Unell 1992: 31). It will be argued that even if one child is protected then the costs have been well incurred. On the other hand there is always the danger that it is the organisation that is more concerned to be seen to be checking rather than any rational account being taken of the efficiency of checks.

This fear that we may be confusing "the safety of the child ... with the safety of the organisation" (Unell 1992: 105) is further underlined by the American legal theory of the 'negligent hiring doctrine'. This doctrine requires employers to exercise due care in the recruitment and selection of employees and if the employee holds a position of special trust, such as the care of children, then the employer should have been on notice that selection should include an investigation of the prospective employee's background, including, where possible a criminal history record check.

The interpreting of the relevance of a previous conviction has already been signalled as potentially problematic. Whilst offences against children may be clear enough, the disclosure of other convictions may be more open to variation in their interpretation. A 'common sense' approach may rule out a person from employment with one agency but not from another willing to make a more liberal decision on the same information. With discretion to the decision makers on the one hand and limited rights of appeal to applicants on the other, the opportunities are lessened for any notions of natural justice.

Whether or not these selection decisions become more sophisticated a new expertise in making them will be claimed. The position begins to mirror the moves we have seen in other areas of child protection in the community, to pursue inter-agency cooperation, information exchange and decisions made by child protection specialist workers (see eg. Dept. of Health 1991 (a)).

We have described elsewhere this move to a 'politics of protection' where the collation of more and more information is seen as an unmitigated good in itself and develops its own momentum that becomes impossible to resist (Thomas and Hebenton 1991b). A move from a 'need to know' to a 'need to nose', but in a context that makes the meaning of 'protection' by no means self-explanatory. The state having once held a clear 'protective' role towards its more vulnerable members is now using the concept in a number of seemingly disparate discourses, whereby the notion of being 'at risk' can be applied to children, elderly people, families, neighbourhoods and communities. In so doing 'protection' has arguably become a metaphor for societies trying to realign the relationship between the individual society and the state.

Outside of this build up of momentum towards 'protection' critical discussion becomes marginalised. The concept of the 'dangerous' person, for example, becomes a question of 'common sense' identification from a previous criminal record that is 'self-evident'. Arguments that suggest alternatives to a 'common-sense' approach bring with them far more imponderables eg:

> "Many of those who commit the most serious crimes against persons tend to have lived normal lives in the community, and to be without a record. For them the question who might be dangerous cannot be asked".
>
> (Bowden 1985: 270)

Questions of race or gender become equally liable to marginalisation. Vetting procedures which make no distinction between the sex of the applicant, conveniently avoid any discussion of the reason why the perpetrators of crimes against children are predominantly male. In 1989, for example, 98 per cent of sexual offences in England and Wales were committed by men (Home Office 1990). Vetting regardless of race, runs a further danger of compounding the racism that is already resulting in an over-representation of black people in the criminal justice system and therefore over-representation of the number of black people with a criminal record (see eg. Gordon 1988: NACRO 1986).

The rehabilitation of former offenders is also placed to one side by the increase in vetting. The need to protect children militates against notions of 'spent' offences or 'going straight'. In the USA criticism of rehabilitation schemes have become lodged around the 'what works?' paradigm and the growth of interest in the rights of victims of crime rather than the offenders (see eg. US Dept. of Justice 1988: 43-49), whilst similar themes can be traced in the UK and Western Europe where criminality is seen as "increasingly disconnected from the broader structure of class and power, and increasingly re-located into a psycho-dynamic theory of maladjustment" (Taylor 1981: 74). Courses of treatment aimed at child sex offenders aimed at 'containment' rather than cure in the 'common sense' interest of saying certain people's access to children must always be monitored.

As regards the children themselves the moves to protection can be seen as complementary to raising awareness of children's rights. The UK Children Act 1989, for example, lays great emphasis on the need to take children's views into account and to make proper complaints and representation procedures for children to voice their concerns. Such moves begin to recognise the importance of status and power rather than just age, as being a determinant of child protection (see eg. Howard League 1985: 128), but they also avoid issues such as childrens sexuality and their right to a sexual life of their own (see eg. Brongersma 1988).

7 Criminal records – The future

In this concluding chapter, our task is twofold: first, to outline the likely trajectory for the maintenance and disclosure of criminal records here in the UK, and to contextualize it by examining the major factors that will, in our view, both impinge on and shape this trajectory. Second, to seek to understand, at the general level, why criminal record systems have assumed their present configuration and to suggest a future research agenda.

The Home Office 1991 Scrutiny

In our account of the contemporary UK criminal records systems (chapter 3), we examined the fragmented nature of the system and looked at other criticisms that had been aimed at its operation. In particular, we outlined the working of the National Identification Bureau and the Police National Computer, the local record offices and the emerging National Criminal Intelligence Service. Much of the criticism of existing arrangements was focused through the 1990 Home Affairs Committee report *Criminal Records* which the Government responded to in July 1990. Part of that response was to set in motion a Home Office 'efficiency scrutiny' of the national criminal record system. The terms of reference of the efficiency scrutiny were:

"i.   to review the present arrangements at national and local level for the funding, maintenance and disclosure of the National Collection of Criminal Records, to determine whether they enable an efficient and effective service to be provided;

ii.   to identify the present and potential scope of the national collection, and any implications for local force records of possible changes in the scope;

iii.   to examine current practice in providing access to and disclosure from the collection, to make proposals for any changes in the principles governing access and disclosure and to specify their likely effects; and

iv.   to make recommendations on the future management and resourcing of the national collection including arrangements for the supply of information to the collection and the disclosure of information from it".

(Hansard 28th November 1990 col. 418)

The Scrutiny Report, as it became known, was submitted to the Home Secretary in April 1991, and published in October 1991. Many of the criticisms previously made by the Home Affairs Committee were endorsed, with the current system of criminal record keeping described as being "in a very unsatisfactory state" (Home Office 1991: para.19).

In making its recommendations, it was also clear that the Home Office was using the Scrutiny Report to set the future of the national criminal record firmly within the context of the overall computerization of the UK criminal justice system (see also chapter 4). The Home Office chaired Committee for the Coordination of Computerization in the Criminal Justice System (CCCJS) had been in existence for sometime but the Scrutiny Report was an opportunity to reaffirm the key role of the national criminal record system in the CCCJS process (Home Office 1991: para.34) and that "the CCCJS should be the main determinant of priorities" over the future strategic plans being drawn up (Home Office 1991: para.43).

Although the contributors to the CCCJS include representatives from the crown courts, magistrates courts, probation service and prison service, we might expect that the police, with their much larger involvement in using information technology, will take a more than active role in directing the future goals of the CCCJS (see Newing 1990).

Within the context of the CCCJS, the Scrutiny Report expects future plans to be determined by three factors:

1.   The entire collection should be held on a single computerized system.

2   The computer system should permit searching on characteristics other than name in order to exploit the investigative potential of the records.

3.   Records should be circulated and up-dated electronically by means of links to other criminal justice system agencies, picking up the information as close to source as possible.

The long-term recommendations of the Scrutiny Report can be viewed in three sections, namely –

a.   concerning the system as such

b.   the management of the system

c.   the future of disclosures of criminal records for vetting purposes.

We consider these recommendations below, and then briefly note other short-term recommendations made by the Scrutiny team.

The new record system

The Report made recommendations that a new National Criminal Records System (NCRS) should be created and held in computerized form on the Police National Computer. This new integrated record would expand the national system to an estimated 8 million records, by transferring all local records on to it. All local record offices would be closed in the interests of avoiding duplication and cutting costs, and all those non-reportable offences, cautions and bind-overs previously held at local level, transferred to the NCRS. A degree of 'weeding' could take place during the process to ensure that information is only held to facilitate the three purposes of investigation, judicial purpose and vetting, and Her Majesty's Inspectorate of Constabulary would be expected to prevent local criminal record offices from "regerminating" (Home Office 1991: para.59).

The exact content of the record would need to be considered by the police and in particular the Police National Computer Organization having oversight of the PNC. Notable problems were signalled with the judicial purpose for which records were needed in Crown Courts, where a degree of variation had been experienced in the past as to how much detail courts wanted on antecedent reports; the impact of the Criminal Justice Act 1991 had also to be considered in this regard (see chapter 4). The Scrutiny Report suggests that the new standardized NCRS being proposed might not allow for variation and suggested talks be entered into with the courts to reach an agreement on a standard form of antecedents.

The idea of splitting records into 'hard' criminal history elements and 'soft' intelligence for investigative purposes was rejected "for practical and technical reasons" (Home Office 1991: para.70). The softer information currently held via the NIB74 form, will, it is proposed go on to the PNC (see also Home Office 1991: para.52).

The criminal history element of the NCRS would also ideally include a record of dates of custody whether on remand or under-sentence, including periods of parole or licence. The record would include the duration of suspended sentences, disqualifications and periods on bail. It was also suggested that an automatic facility to identify and mark 'spent' convictions would be helpful.

The Scrutiny team spent some time considering the matter of 'weeding' records in order not to overburden the system. The Report recognized that the police service had an "instinctive inclination...to keep criminal records for a long time." (Home Office 1991: para.79) and cited the previously agreed ACPO guidelines on this issue: retention for 20 years since the last offence or age 70, whichever comes first (see ACPO 1987 for full details). The Report called for Home Office/ACPO consultation to ensure sufficient 'weeding' occurred at the interim stage of computerization, but with a long term strategy to be based on empirical research, such research results allowing for the development of a more discriminating approach to 'weeding' of records.

Managing the new record system

A number of options for the future management of the NCRS were considered in the Report, including contracting out and privatization.

In the end it recommended the introduction of a new National Criminal Records Agency (NCRA) under the sponsorship of the Home Secretary and with its own statutory advisory committee and chief executive. The Home Secretary would be given the power to statutorily define a criminal record and give legal guidelines on their maintenance. The NCRA would be financially self-supporting by being able to charge for disclosures to agencies requiring a vetting service. NCRA would monitor uses of the NCRS and ensure efficient running of the system on a day to day basis, and evaluate any need for change including changes in technology.

The future disclosure arrangements

The Scrutiny Report stated its misgivings about the current arrangements for disclosing criminal records for vetting purposes. It described existing policies as being confused and uncomfortably shared between the police and the Home Office, coverage as being fragmented and variable between different geographic areas in the UK, and procedures as inconsistent – whereby, for example, some police forces check previous address as far back as 5 years, while others check back 20 years. Add to this the variations in interpreting record content by recipients (see chapters 5 and 6) and it is only too obvious why concern has been expressed over the nature of vetting arrangements.

The Report weighed up the arguments for more restrictions on vetting, against the argument for having no restrictions and making records entirely 'open' – as they are at the point of entry into court record. It came down in favour of a continuance of present policies based on selective disclosures for vetting made against a presumption of confidentiality. This, despite a recognition of an "ever widening demand for vetting" (Home Office 1991: para.142) which should be taken into account if ever there was a need to legislate to prescribe the scope of vetting (Home Office 1991: para.186).

What was finally proposed was a status quo position until computerization had taken place and after new procedural safeguards for national security and probity vetting with vetting also being available for licensing or 'fit and proper person' requirements acknowledged by Parliament. Vetting of those with 'substantial access' to children was to continue, with yet another examination of the definition of 'substantial access', whilst vetting was also to become available to other vulnerable groups including the elderly and mentally disordered. The Report suggested that the Driver and Vehicle Licensing Agency could divert some work away from the proposed NCRA by taking over the vetting of taxi-drivers.

More specifically, the Report recommended two forms of vetting. Vetting in respect of children, national security and probity in the administration of justice would be subject to 'special disclosure' including all 'spent' convictions. The other form of vetting it described as 'ordinary disclosure', which would apply to all other cases (Home Office 1991: para.150) and would not allow for 'spent' convictions to be disclosed. Cautions would only appear on a 'special disclosure' case. Interestingly, the Report suggests that in cases involving older and less vulnerable children, then 'ordinary disclosure' may apply.

In the context of previous discussion earlier in the book, it is important to note that on the matter of enforced subject access (see chapter 3), the Report agreed with the UK Data Protection Registrar that "this is a thoroughly undesirable practice" (Home Office 1991: para.176) but the Report did not propose any immediate action to make such a practice a criminal offence; it is suggested that the position on enforced subject access be reviewed after the computerization of criminal records is complete.

At the time of writing, all these recommendations are being considered by the Home Office, including the idea of a distinct vetting agency located within the NCRA, to advise on assessing the relevance of disclosed offences. A draft circular revising Home Office circular No.102/1988 on the vetting of those with substantial access to children was issued for consultation in July 1992 (see chapter 6).

However, the Government, in making its interim reply to the Report in October 1991, anticipated that the computerization of the criminal record would not be complete before the mid-1990s. In the meantime, the expansion of the records was accepted with the exception of 'bind overs' being added in; the Government wanted more time to reach a view on this. The creation of a central agency to manage records for the benefit of the whole criminal justice system was agreed and the position of disclosure arrangements was to be the subject of a consultation document later in 1992 (*Hansard* 22nd October 1991 cols 533-534).

Before concluding this section, it is worth noting that while the Report indicates the path for strategic development, it also makes a number of short-term recommendations which the Government hope will lead to immediate improvements in the maintenance and processing of records. These recommendations include the abandoning of the old NIB micro-fiche collection for post-1980 offenders - with all this information now being back-converted and going onto the PNC conviction history file. To improve the problem of delays in input of information to the NIB, it was decided that NIB74A's should be sent off within 5 days of an arrest to give notice of a pending prosecution and NIB74B's within 13 days of a court decision (see chapter 3 for previous concerns on these matters). Ideas were also suggested to improve the quality of antecedents presented in court, in terms of legibility of reply, numbers of copies to relevant parties, and reaffirmation of the position that acquittals were to be clearly marked as such, and not cited as convictions. All of these short-term changes were to be overseen by a newly created advisory board for the NIB (Home Office 1991: para.107 and Annex M). The implementation of these recommendations through the proposed advisory board has yet to occur (personal communication with NIB August 1992).

The European information field

Our view is that the trajectory for development of the criminal record in the UK is likely to influenced in the medium term by three issues: trends in police and criminal justice co-operation in Europe; developing data protection concerns; and migration, particularly related to harmonization of regulated employment within the European Community.

Faced with the increasing internationalization of crime, national governments and their police have devoted much effort to developing co-operative counter-measures, and further evolution is under way through the machinery of conventions and 'arrangements' which we describe below. The international policy space for these departures is now additionally crowded by recent talk of more embracing systems of European policing, such as Europol, and also by both sectoral and bilateral arrangements.

A central part in these initiatives is played by the attempt to develop adequate information systems across national and jurisdictional borders. This extends, what we can call the 'informatization' of the police, to the inter-governmental level in all European countries. This, we would argue, is also part of a more general trend towards bringing information and communication technology to bear upon administrative activities in the public sphere (see Taylor and Williams 1991). Much of the development of 'informatized' police work is nationally and internationally slow and piecemeal at the moment, but there are signs that the pace is quickening under various pressures from international agreements like the completion of the European Community Single Market, and more parochially the UK-France Channel Tunnel Protocol. Baxter (1990: 198-224) notes the increasing importance of information in police work. The importance of rapidly communicated, secure, accessible and ample information to the goals of policing across borders is likely to stimulate further the harmonization or integration of information systems, and perhaps their eventual supranational centralization; a tendency, we have argued that is evident within countries, of which the movement towards more rationalized and centralized criminal records and criminal intelligence in the UK is a case in point.

We have come a long way from those first hesitant steps to introduce a criminal record collection in the UK to compensate for the loss of the 'facility' of transporting people to the antipodes (see chapter 2). Changes have taken place in both the means of maintaining criminal records, and in particular the growth of information technology that enables easier storage and more rapid retrieval, and the uses to which a criminal record collection is put. Disclosure of criminal records to agencies outside of the criminal justice system is growing constantly to feed an apparently insatiable demand.

In Western Europe we have witnessed the coming together of the member states of the European Community in ever closer forms of inter-governmental cooperation and tentative steps toward political union. The original Maastricht Treaty on Political Union drawn up in December 1991, included provisions for cooperation in the spheres of justice and home affairs, and made manifest some of the ideas that had been germinating for a European Police Office or Europol. Central to this idea of Europol was the exchange of personal information between the police authorities of the Community and including "measures relating to further training, research, forensic matters and 'criminal records departments'" (European Commission 1991: Annex to Article A (8); emphasis added).

It should also be noted that the broad regulatory context within which the Europol initiative is situated is itself in some respects favourable to structural change. The Maastricht Treaty brings the whole area of justice and home affairs co-operation closer to the mainstream of the European Community. Thus, quite apart from the specific domain of police co-operation, the member states are directed to regard as of "common interest policies on combatting crime and illegal immigration", as well as matters falling under the rubric of judicial co-operation in criminal matters.

The Maastricht Treaty was only placing on the table that which had been mooted for some time by the deliberations of the so-called TREVI group. This group, named after the fountain in Rome, consists of 6 monthly meetings of ministers, civil servants and senior police officers of the EC member states. Formed in 1976 it has provided a forum for the analysis of "policing Europe", with working parties examining terrorism, public order drug-trafficking and related issues. At its June 1990 Dublin meeting the TREVI group produced a "Programme of Action" which had highlighted amongst other things the need for a Community wide "development of a common information system designed to collect data and descriptions of persons and objects." The Maastricht meeting of the European Council had adopted this idea for a European Information System (EIS) and deliberations were opened as to whether its permanent central siting would be in Rome, Wiesbaden or Lyon.

The significance of Lyon as a central point for the proposed EIS, lay in its existing role as providing the headquarters for the International Criminal Police Organisation better known as Interpol. Interpol was, in any event, already providing a form of information exchange for police forces throughout Europe whether or not they were members of the European Community, and indeed extended its services to a world-wide network of police organisations. As an estimated 80 per cent of Interpol's work was European based a decision was taken in 1987 to create the European Secretariat or European Liaison Bureau within the Lyon HQ, to coordinate and improve communications between the national Interpol offices or National Central Bureaus throughout the region. At the same time as the Secretariat was established the modernisations of the computer data-banks and allied information technology was also coming to fruition. By the 1990s Interpol had 'state-of-the-art' storage and retrieval technology for information given to it, by its member police authorities (see

Kendall 1989). Central to the new system was the Criminal Information system (CIS) and an Automated Search Facility (ASF) to find images, photographs and fingerprints from its Electronic Archive System.

Interpol and the European Information System of the proposed Europol, were running alongside a third initiative in the Europeanisation of the police. The Schengen Convention had originally been drawn up in 1985 and confirmed in 1990 by Germany, France and the Benelux countries. By the end of 1992 Italy, Spain and Portugal had become signatories. The Schengen Convention provides us with the most complete model we have, of how close inter-governmental cooperation can be incorporated amongst neighbouring national police authorities. It also had within its text the genesis of yet a third system for exchanging personal information held in the police sectors of the component countries: The Schengen Information System.

The Schengen Information System is intended to only contain certain police information supplied by each of the contracting member states. Each nation will have its own data file section which it will be responsible for in terms of supervision. There will also be a central SIS data base held in Strasbourg with oversight coming from a joint supervisory authority, that will act in accordance with the Council of Europe Convention on Data Processing (Council of Europe 1981), the Council of Europe Recommendations on the use of personal information held in the police sector (Council of Europe 1988), the provisions of the French Data Protection laws applicable in Strasbourg, and the Schengen Convention's own provisions (Schengen Convention 1990).

Together the initiatives by Interpol, the TREVI Group and the contracting members of the Schengen Convention have moved, or are moving, the usage of police held personal information on to a European scale of operations.

Of course, beyond the foreground of Maastricht and the more specific roots provided by the other organizational structures like TREVI, there is a more general backdrop of laws, conventions and institutional developments particular to or inclusive of the European Community states in the area of criminal justice co-operation. By far the most significant in relation to criminal records is the Council of Europe's 1959 *European Convention on Mutual Assistance in Criminal Matters,* which was only ratified by the UK in November 1991. Essentially, the Convention lays down procedures which apply to matters of examination of witnesses, experts and persons in custody, and transmissions of information from judicial (criminal) records (see Spencer 1990: 94-6).

There are obligations arising under Articles 13 and 22 of the Convention as regards co-operation between member states on criminal records. According to the Council of Europe, such co-operation could proceed most efficiently, if states agreed a standardized list of offences which would have to be communicated under Article 22 and the establishment of national criminal records which would contain convictions for these offences could also substantially facilitate co-operation in this sphere (see Council of Europe 1984: 50-54 for a detailed discussion of this matter).

There has already been recognition in the UK that greater Europeanization of policing and moves to harmonization will have implications for criminal record maintenance and usage. Indeed, the Home Affairs Committee in considering practical police co-operation in Europe recommended that the UK take the lead in producing a European Community standard in relation to disclosure of criminal records (House of Commons 1990b). Furthermore, the Home Office Scrutiny team commissioned their own synopsis of the situation on criminal records in other Community states as part of its own work, and as we discuss below, the Scrutiny Report raised a number of issues in relation to implications for the UK.

Data protection regimes

We have made reference at various points in this book to the important role of data protection in relation to criminal records. The whole dimension of ever more demands being made on criminal records outside of the criminal justice system, raises a real tension between ideas of confidentiality and privacy. The Home Office described as "dangerous", the practice of relatively low ranking police officers phoning their information and intelligence through to local authority staff concerning child protection matters, but felt they were doing it "with the best of motives" (Home Office 1991: para 155). The Police Complaints Authority has reported "a noticeable increase in the number of complaints about police officers making use of the police national computer or force intelligence records for other than official purposes" and were "rather surprised" to find more senior officers who did not regard it as serious enough to even warrant internal disciplinary proceedings (PCA 1991: 19).

The future of criminal records systems appears to lie in computerisation and ever more efficient storage and retrieval. Data protection measures will be in constant tension with the accumulation and uses of police held information and have been described by the chairman of the Association of Chief Police Officer's International Committee as a "thorny issue" (Birch 1992). The perceived growth in international crime as with the growth of all crime, leads to demands for increasingly sophisticated measures to confront it. The police forces of this country and Europe "have to be given the means by which they could fight fire with fire. That clearly means the transmission of data on criminal records and other information very quickly indeed" (House of Commons 1990b: para 84).

Interestingly, the 1991 Scrutiny Report's recognition of the need to provide a statutory basis for the UK criminal record system – setting out its scope, purpose and content – was no doubt informed by the need to have a legal basis to such a system. Without that basis, there would be no protection for the vetting process and other uses of the system against the risk of challenge of alleged interference with the right to privacy under Article 8 of the *European Convention on Human Rights*.

The general pattern of data protection arrangements across Europe reveals a highly ambiguous message (see Nugter 1990) and specific data protection measures on police held data consists of much that is piecemeal at the European level. However, it has been accepted by most commentators that the most appropriate 'route' for data protection is through the legislative process of the European Community. A text for data protection at the European level has only recently been placed on the table (see Commission of the European Communities 1990). This 1990 European Commission Draft Directive has had a protracted career through the European Parliament, with a heavily amended version approved on the 11th March 1992, but with its future shape still to be determined by the Commission and the Council of Ministers.

The Draft Directive, in attempting to resolve the failures of previous Council of Europe conventions on data protection, introduces many novel features. Thus, it not only embraces the tightest provisions of each member state, along with international norms, but deals with new ones - the proposed extension to manual data processing is a case in point. The Draft makes it an offence to make the access of one's personal data file a precondition of employment - tackling thereby the problem of enforced subject access (see chapter 3). In addition, data that falls into the 'sensitive' category (and in most states that includes criminal records) are prohibited from electronic processing except with the express, written consent of the subject or where, on public interest grounds, a member state has permitted it *under a specific statute* that embodies safeguards (see Commission of the European Communities 1990: Article 17). The same Article also forbids data on criminal convictions to be held outside public sector files; this is contrary to current UK practice, and broaches the vexed question of employers holding such information as a result of vetting. This subject was explored by the Home Affairs Committee in 1989 and 1990 and on two separate occasions formed part of the evidence to it by the UK Data Protection Registrar (see House of Commons 1990a, 1990b). It is also dealt with in the current Code of Practice for police (ACPO 1987), where, however, it is not clear how far the Code may prevent such disclosures outside the public sector in view of the police's ability to avail themselves of certain procedures in the registration of their data (see Spencer 1990: 64). Spencer (1990) argues that the ACPO Code is weaker on this matter that the Council of Europe's Recommendation (87)15 on police data, which places tighter case-by-case restrictions around disclosures of this kind than does the Code. The Draft Directive's blanket proscription on disclosures from police records is at odds with the UK Data Protection Registrar's preference for specific safeguards and for wider public policies on access to criminal records in order to deal with abuses concerning such disclosures.

It is important to note that while it is unclear how far such provisions will relate to areas outside Community law, member states are being asked to extend the principles of the Draft directive to those public sector areas such as police and criminal justice.

It remains to be seen how things will develop, and one can only agree with David Flaherty's description of the core problem:

"There are clear limits to the power of a data protection authority, if a government is determined to introduce a practice that may be, at least in part". (Flaherty 1986a)

What is clear, in our view, is that deliberations and appraisals of the status of data protection in the midst of new departures continues in various fora and informally amongst the policy community. In November 1991 the Data Protection Commissioners from Belgium, Denmark, France, Germany, United Kingdom, Ireland, Luxembourg and the Netherlands met in the Hague to discuss the privacy implications of growing European police cooperation. They issued a joint statement calling for adequate legislative privacy protection in all the developments taking place and particularly the Schengen Information System (Statewatch 1992). The UK Data Protection Registrar had already outlined his wider views on data protection in the European Community to a similar meeting in Wiesbaden (Data Protection Registrar 1991: 48-54). The trajectory of data protection will continue to shape discussion on matters of criminal record data quality and communication to third parties.

Migration and employment

In terms of population structure, growth and large-scale movement of people, Europe in the 1990s and 21st century looks set for major upheaval. In the 1980s, the previous decade's immigration trend of family re-unification gave way to a new phenomenon - mass refugee applications. Following Eastern Europe's revolutions at the end of 1989 there has been considerable population movement into Western Europe, notably Germany. Southern Europe (Greece, Spain, Italy and Portugal), formerly countries of emigration, has in the last few years received major flows of immigrants largely from North Africa (see Baldwin-Edwards 1991). Demographic changes display a marked contrast between the developed nations of Europe and the impoverished economies of North Africa. Low birth rates across the entire European Community have set Europe on a path of increasing old age dependency ratios (pensioners/workers) along with older and possibly insufficient workforces. North Africa, on the other hand, is set for population explosion over the next few decades.

By the end of the 1980s, foreign workers recruited to fill labour shortages has become a significant feature in Europe, and the exchange of labour among member states of the European Community has been developing from a direct legal and political basis (see Molle 1990: 201-221). When harmonization of employment measures and regulation of occupational structures across the European Community is linked to the numbers of people at any one time with a criminal record (see chapter 5), it is clear that policies and practices on disclosure from criminal records may be of great significance.

The Home Office has been urged to promote a common EC standard for the use of the criminal record for vetting purposes (House of Commons 1990 (b)). The whole question of a more integrated Europe with a free movement of labour brings with it a series of questions that are only beginning to be addressed. The Home Office Scrutiny Report's own survey of practice throughout the European Community revealed the issues starkly.

The extent of the disclosure of criminal records outside of the criminal justice system is subject to wide variations. In the Republic of Ireland no disclosures are made with regard to employment vetting. Italy, on the other hand, allows very wide access and makes records available to employers provided they can give reasonable grounds for their enquiry.

On disclosure from the record for positions with substantial access to children, practice is notably dissimilar to the UK system, with the possible exception of Denmark. As mentioned in chapter 6, the Association of Directors of personal social services, has argued for thought to be given "to the protocols required for synchronisation of information requirements with the European Community" and communication between European employers and police forces to be given a priority (ADSS 1992: para 18).

It is our view that pressures in this area will considerably determine the future shape of disclosure policy but within the overall framework of the UK's Scrutiny Report.

Towards an understanding...

How can one best try and understand the growth and nature of criminal record systems? To detail such an understanding is an ambitious project – our object here can only be to suggest conceptual pointers that may be useful in guiding a way towards the goal of that project.

As the growing body of historical studies of technology demonstrates, the relationship between technology, technological innovation and change, and social life is so immensely complex as to defy all except the easy and, in the end, empirically uninformative generalization (see Yearley 1988). However, we feel that there is an obligation to 'theorize' at this point – if only to preserve the sanity of the authors!

The key ideas for our analysis are drawn from the work of Giddens on the central role of surveillance and bureaucracy in modern societies (see for example Giddens 1987) and Poggi on the nature of the state (see Poggi 1990). We draw on their frameworks.

Criminal records, surveillance and modernity

In modern societies, rational bureaucracy – whether private or public – is ubiquitous, and it appears to some of us as a 'tyranny of convenience' (Dworkin 1990). Without it, few of the routine features of contemporary life would be possible: including the provision of policing and social welfare. Today, it can be argued, that one of the most obvious indicators of the pervasiveness of bureaucracy is the huge expansion of personal documentary information which is held by state agencies.

Criminal records are the case in point

This context of bureaucracy was, of course, Max Weber's bleak and ironic view of modernity as that of being enclosed in an administrative 'iron cage'. The idea of bureaucracy as a highly rationalized mode of information gathering and administrative control has been taken up most magisterially in recent times by the late Michel Foucault (see for example Foucault 1979) and more recently still by Anthony Giddens. They have discussed the administrative logic of modernity in terms of the growth of 'surveillance', here to be understood as a means of administrative power rather than in the narrow sense of 'spying'. Modern rational bureaucracy, of which the state's criminal record- keeping capacity is an exemplar, is in this analysis a highly effective and durable mode of surveillance. What is required at the analytic level is to connect the nature of surveillance with the phenomena of information and bureaucracy.

Rule (1973) helps us to structure our thinking on this through his concept of the composition of the surveillance system: the first entails a "means of knowing when rules are being obeyed, when they are broken, and most importantly who is responsible for which" (Rule ibid: 21-3). The second requires an "ability to locate and identify those responsible for misdeeds of some kind" (ibid). One must examine both the internal dynamics of the surveillance system and its relationship to the social structure.

Criminal record systems qua surveillance systems grow, but they do not grow just as they please (to paraphrase Marx). The evident growth of criminal records attested to in previous chapters is subject to regular constraints, both from inside the system and from the social context in which it is embedded. On the internal dynamics of such systems, Rule's analytic criteria for examining change in such systems is of value (Rule ibid: 269-277). He points to: first, the development of surveillance capacity. On such developing capacity, criminal record systems are no exception. The dimensions of capacity all show signs of increase – size, data growth per individual, centralization. The advantages of such capacity growth are also clear to something like criminal record systems, which have to act as aid to the 'administrative' decisions on large populations, and ensure these decisions are related to past behaviour of individuals. It is advantageous to such systems to develop the maximum possible surveillance capacity.

While Rule's analysis of the expansionist dynamic has value, others have suggested that it is to symbolic politics that one must look for a more complete understanding of policy strategy. Gordon (1990), for example, highlights the fact that in the USA, "criminal justice entrepreneurs have been able to manipulate traditional law enforcement symbols of public protection, modern visions of the unmitigated good of unlimited information, and broader images of the US political system to support a virtually unregulated, centralized crime information system", (Gordon ibid: 78). Her analysis of the situation in the USA relies on examining the competition of symbols. Gordon argues that interacting forces of federalization and elite influence in the administration of justice are key to a policy understanding, but also related to the realization that computers as apolitical tools for rationally improving systems has been supplemented by the conclusion that such computer applications constitute a kind of 'reinforcement politics' that serves the values and status of those in charge. The development of the criminal record system in the USA bears out this perspective – early endorsements of central control of record keeping are reinforced by the technological superiority of the FBI, the new class of information managers in the FBI and the state record repositories, and the increased capacity of criminal justice officials to provide technical support to other government agencies and to mayors and governors. This patina of technical expertise exercises, according to Gordon, persuasive pressure for central expansion and innovation (Gordon ibid: 81).

Apart from the issue of capacity itself, it is equally important to try and understand what factors are shaping the system. As an example, let us look at non-criminal justice use of records. Here, Laudon (1986) identifies four broad factors related to this matter: social, organizational, technological and legal or regulatory. The social factors most frequently cited as causes of the growing use of records for employment purposes are crime and economic development. Both factors increase demand, it could be argued, by organizations for criminal records access. On this logic, in high crime areas, employers face a greater risk that applicants will have a criminal background. In economically advanced states, inter-organizational dependencies mushroom and exchanges of information among organizations can reduce uncertainties. In addition, in economically advanced states, the labour force is characterized by labour structures having positions involving 'responsible trust'.

Several organizational factors are related to the supply and cost of criminal records. In the USA, states which received large amounts of federal funding through the LEAA developed more comprehensive and advanced systems than states that received less. In some states of the USA, the state government exercises significant central budgetary control over local agencies, thus rationalizing record practices in the state and making access to centralized files more efficient. In addition, some US states centralized and automated their record systems before others; over time, automated data became targets for potential user groups previously discouraged from using certain records because they were dispersed and difficult to access. The leading technological factor to consider, one can argue, is whether the state operates a computerized system. Such systems can respond more rapidly and efficiently to requests from employers. Hence, such use is expected to be greater in such states.

A last feature to consider is the regulatory milieu in which criminal record systems operate. It is argued that in USA states with express prohibitions against the use of criminal records in the employment relationship, and in states characterized by a regulatory 'regime', the use of records in employment will be less common than in those states without these strong 'regimes'. However, others have convincingly made the case that privacy and related regulations merely legitimize existing patterns of disclosure by transferring value issues to matters of 'efficiency' criteria, and in so doing may actually increase disclosure of records:

"By this criterion, privacy is deemed protected if three conditions are met in managing personal data:
1. that the data be kept accurate, complete, up-to-date, and subject to review and correction by the persons concerned;
2. that the uses of filed data proceed according to rules of due process that data subjects can know, and if necessary, invoke;

3. that the organization collecting and using personal data do so only in-so-far as necessary to attain their appropriate organizational goals. Under these principles, organizations can claim to protect the privacy of the persons with whom they deal, even as they accumulate more and more data on those persons and greater and greater power over their lives. It would be difficult to imagine a more advantageous interpretation of privacy protection, from the standpoint of surveillance organizations".

(Rule *et al* 1980: 74)

In one of the very few studies on the relative strength of these broad factors, Laudon (1986) used the results from a forty state survey of non-criminal justice usage. He examined five correlates of usage: crime, income (per capita), federal funds, centralization and age of the system. Although these variables are also highly inter-correlated, Laudon found that from regression analysis he could eliminate two of the variables early on - age and per capita income. Focusing on the remaining three, the final results suggested that crime rate and federal funding are the most important long-range variables in non-criminal justice usage, and that centralization is the most important system characteristic. Laudon found, therefore, that crime rate was the most powerful factor in such usage. Perhaps the most interesting findings concern regulations - here Laudon found that state and federal regulations have had little or no impact on the overall level of employment usage.

Returning to the more general level, it is clear that in modern society, surveillance is a constitutive attribute. The modern state's surveillance capacities are produced by the use of rational bureaucracy for the administrative penetration of society. As Giddens and Poggi have argued, this development suggests a particular meaning for the separation between state and society (Giddens 1981: 169-81; Poggi 1978: 92-116). The modern state is separated from society in respect of the emergence of a public power from pre-existing 'king based' regimes. However, from an administrative point of view, pre-modern states and their rulers were far more separated from their societies than are their modern counterparts. They could not subject their populations to the fine mesh of bureaucratic surveillance evident in modern society.

The development of criminal record systems, as expressions of bureaucratic surveillance, is an important component of what Cohen has referred to as the "increasing involvement of the state in the business of deviancy control" (Cohen 1985: 13). Whereas cercarial regimes such as the prison and asylum prefigured as expressions of the growth of bureaucratic surveillance and the power of the state, a number of writers have pointed to the fact that in the organized modern state, society itself becomes the disciplinary mechanism (see for example Melossi 1976). In that context, criminal record systems which incorporate both exclusionary and inclusionary strategies at the same moment, may be seen to perform a kind of instrumental discipline.

Research agendas

We have argued in this book for the importance of studying contemporary criminal record systems both in their own terms and as a window on a wider landscape. While in our view criminal record systems in modern society throw up several research agendas, it is important to start by recognizing that there has been a research vacuum. One commentator, writing in the context of the USA in the late 1980s has noted that:

> "One billion dollars and fifteen years after a national computerized criminal history was proposed in 1968, answers to a number of significant questions are still not known:
>
> - Would a national CCH prevent the pretrial release on bail of criminals with a prior record, and, if so, in how many cases?
>
> - Does a national CCH represent a significant enhancement over existing state CCH systems...?
>
> - Would a national CCH significantly alter the sentencing behaviour of criminal court magistrates and, if so, by how many additional weeks, months, years? (How do criminal court magistrates use criminal history information?)
>
> - In 1980, there were 9 million arrests for all kinds of offenses by law enforcement agencies in the United States. Would a national CCH lead to an increase in the number of arrests, and if so, by how much? (Is criminal history information useful in the apprehension of criminals?)...
>
> Nowhere in the historical record of the FBI, LEAA congressional testimony and statements, or public announcements, is there evidence that these questions were even considered or answers attempted".
>
> (Laudon 1986: 350)

The Council of Europe has also highlighted the dearth of research studies (see Council of Europe 1984: 48-9).

Research on criminal records has, in our view, to be seen as operating at three levels. At the most specific level, it is important that domain related studies are undertaken. Here, we refer to studies that attempt to examine direct policy-oriented questions in relation to criminal record maintenance or use. For example, in the UK in the employment domain, there is a pressing need to analyse the nature of decision-making processes following criminal record disclosure to local authorities in child protection and on those with substantial access to children. Similarly, there is a need for comparative European-wide research on Certificates of Good Conduct (which contain a wide disparity of criminal history information) and employment. Other valuable work could be undertaken in this domain in relation to the practice of 'licensing' - what is, for example, the impact of criminal convictions where applicants are seeking liquor licences? (see Manchester 1990).

At the second level, research needs to confront the issue of the social impact of current and proposed criminal record systems. The purpose of research at this level is to describe the ways in which life for the modern 'citizen' is affected by such systems. Clearly, there are several variables which mediate any such social impact studies, such as the technical architecture of the system. But, that aside, social impact analysis could focus on: organizational process and decision-making - how does the criminal records system affect the flow of information within and among criminal justice agencies, patterns of decision-making, and the operations, processes, and programmes of these agencies? As important, how does the system affect non-criminal justice use? Such an analysis could also consider the impact on group and institutional relationships - the types of relationship may include the problem of equity or equal opportunities, the balance of forces within the criminal justice sector, the relationship between citizens, police and technology (see Ackroyd et al 1992). Finally, it could also consider precisely what social value changes are implied by the current configuration of criminal records. At one level, the need is to examine specific value impacts within the criminal justice sector. For example, on punishment - prediction studies on the use, if any, of the criminal record on determinations of prosecution and sentencing; on the concept of rehabilitation. But also impact on social and political values. Questions raised may include, for example, accountability. Clearly with information systems there are at least three versions of accountability – the technical, the legal and finally the political. Research could begin to unravel the complex interrelationships of these three versions and examine how likely any one is to be 'achieved'. There is also the matter of public confidence or trust in the system.

At this second level, one should also place research on policy choices. Dependent on the results of a social impact analysis, one may wish to know if there are public policies which would maximize the benefits of a configured criminal records system but minimize unwanted 'side-effects'. The kind of policy choice scenario referred to in the UK Home Office Scrutiny report is a case in point (Home Office 1991).

At the third level, we would hope for considerations of criminal records as an expression of bureaucratic surveillance and the implications of such for contemporary social analysis. Such a consideration might turn to the prospects of modern societies in what is clearly an 'age of surveillance'. In that context, such work will tackle: the relationships between knowledge of someone's past and the disciplinary power of such knowledge in modern societies.

Conclusion

If research followed on all these three levels we would be well satisfied. As it is, our intention in writing this book is to make more transparent the world of criminal records. However, having said that, we must also sound a further note. Modernity, if it is characterized by anything, is a recognition of the notion of 'reflexivity'. We are acutely aware that it is important to be reflexive about academic contributions to developments in social policy. Intellectual reconstructions of the political programmes behind social control developments, or of the logic-in-use of criminal justice systems, may systematically distort them, typically endowing them with more coherence than they possess. There may in fact be a 'looseness' about criminal records that supports incompatible justifications. That aside, it may be no bad thing in the end, if we reallocate resources to develop and underwrite less information-intensive ways of dealing with people. In other words, if in the context of bureaucratic surveillance, we tried the move to an alternative, looser and more private world.

However, we think it more apt, given the likely outcome, to end by quoting Alexander Solzhenitsyn's description of the work of his fictional character Rusanov - the records administrator:

" It was a job that went by different names in different institutions, but the substance of it was always the same. Only ignoramuses and uninformed outsiders were unaware what subtle, meticulous work it was, what talent it required. It was a form of poetry not yet mastered by the poets themselves. As every man goes through life he fills in a number of forms for the record, each containing a number of questions. A man's answer to one question on one form becomes a little thread, permanently connecting him to the centre...There are thus hundreds of little threads radiating from every man, millions of threads in all. If these threads were suddenly to become visible, the whole sky would look like a spider's web, and if they materialized as elastic bands, buses, trams and even people would lose the ability to move, and the wind would be unable to carry torn-up newspapers or autumn leaves along the streets of the city. They are not visible, they are not material, but every man is constantly aware of their existence. The point is that a completely clean record was almost unattainable, an ideal, like absolute truth. Something negative or suspicious can always be noted down against any man alive. Everyone is guilty of something or has something to conceal. All one has to do is to look hard enough to find out what it is".

(Solzhenitsyn 1971: 208).

Annex

EXCEPTIONS TO THE REHABILITATION OF OFFENDERS ACT 1974

I   EXCEPTIONS MADE BY THE REHABILITATION OF OFFENDERS ACT 1974 (Exceptions) ORDER 1975

A. Offices and Employments

1. Judicial appointments.

2. Employment in the office of the Director of Public Prosecutions.

3. Employment in the office of Procurator Fiscal or District Court Prosecutor or in the Crown Office.

4. Justices' clerks and justices' clerks' assistants, and their equivalent in Scotland.

5. Constables, police cadet, military, naval and air force police, and certain posts involving police work or assisting the police.

6. Employment in the prison service, including appointment to a Board of Visitors or, in Scotland, to a Visiting Committee.

7. Traffic wardens.

8. Probation Officers.

9. Any office or employment concerned with the provision to persons aged under 18 of accommodation, care, leisure and recreational facilities, schooling, social services, supervision or training, being office of employment of such a kind as to enable the holder to have access in the course of his normal duties of which are carried out wholly or partly on the premises where such provision takes place. (As amended by the Rehabilitation of Offenders Act 1974 (Exceptions) (Amendment) Order 1986).

10. Employment connected with the provision of social services which involves access to the young, the old*, the mentally* or physically handicapped*, or the chronic sick* or disabled.*

11. Employment concerned with the provision of health services, within the National Health Service or otherwise, which involves access to patients.*

12. Firearms dealers.

13. Any occupation requiring a licence, certificate, or registration from the Gaming Board for Great Britain.

14. Director, controller or manager of an insurance company.*

15. Any occupation concerned with the management of an abortion clinic or the carrying on of a private hospital or nursing home.*

16. Any occupation concerned with carrying on an establishment for which registration is required by Section 37 of the National Assistance Act 1948 or Section 61 of the Social Work (Scotland) Act 1968.*

17. Any occupation for which a certificate of fitness to keep explosives is required.

18. A person may in certain cases be asked to disclose his spent convictions on the grounds of safeguarding national security.

B. Excepted Professions

1. Medical Practitioner.*

2. Barrister* (in England and Wales) Advocate* (in Scotland) Solicitor.*

3. Chartered accountant*, certified accountant.*

4. Dentist*, dental hygienist*, dental auxiliary.*

   * access to the criminal record for vetting purposes is unlikely to be available in these cases, unless the post involves substantial access to children.

5.   Veterinary surgeon.*

6.   Nurse*, midwife.*

7.   Opthalmic optician*, dispensing optician.*

8.   Pharmaceutical chemist.*

9.   Registered teacher (in Scotland).

10. Any profession to which the Professions Supplementary to Medicine Act 1960 applies and which is undertaken following registration under that Act.*

C.   Excepted Licences, Certificate, Permits and Proceedings

1.   Firearm and shotgun certificates.

2.   Licences which relate to persons under 18 going abroad to perform for profit.*

3.   Certificates to keep explosives for private use.

4.   Proceedings concerned with the admission to or disciplinary action against any member of the excepted professions (above at B).*

5.   Disciplinary proceedings against a constable unlikely to be available in these cases, unless the post involves substantial access to children.

6.   Proceedings before the Gaming Board of Great Britain.

7.   Certain proceedings before a Mental Health Tribunal, Sheriff or the Mental Welfare Commission for Scotland.

* access to the criminal record for vetting purposes is unlikely to be available in these cases, unless the post involves substantial access to children.

8. Certain proceedings concerned with the registration of firearms dealers, the granting, renewal or revocation of firearms certificates, shotgun certificates and other such permits.

9. Proceedings which are concerned with persons under 18 travelling abroad to perform for profit.*

10. Certain proceedings concerned with the approval of appointments in insurance companies*.

11. Certain proceedings concerned with the suitability of those who teach in establishments of further education or are the proprietors of independent schools.

12. Certain proceedings concerned with the control of those licensed to deal in securities.

13. Certain proceedings concerned with the regulation of places involved in abortion and of nursing homes.

14. Certain proceedings concerned with the fitness of those who keep explosives.

15. Proceedings connected with any appeal or review against a decision made under the 1975 Exceptions Order, or other consideration arising from the Order.

* access to the criminal record for vetting purposes is unlikely to be available in these cases, unless the post involves substantial access to children.

II EXCEPTIONS MADE BY THE BANKING ACT 1979

1. Director, controller or manager of a bank. (Made by Section 43 of the Banking Act 1974 by analogy with the exception for directors, controllers or managers of insurance companies).*

2. Certain proceedings concerned with the approval of appointments in banks.

III EXCEPTIONS MADE BY THE REHABILITATION OF OFFENDERS ACT (Exceptions) (Amendment No.2) ORDER 1986.

1. Director or other officer of a building society.*

2. Certain proceedings before the Building Societies Commission.

IV EXCEPTION MADE BY THE FINANCIAL SERVICES ACT 1986

1. Convictions relating to offences of fraud and dishonesty or an offence under legislation concerned with the financial sector in proceedings concerned with the or revocation of authorisation to carry on investment business.*

V EXCEPTION MADE BY THE BANKING ACT 1987

1. Convictions relating to offences of fraud and dishonesty or an offence under legislation relating to the financial sector in proceedings concerned with the granting of or revocation of authorisation to carry on deposit-taking business.*

   * access to the criminal record for vetting purposes is unlikely to be available in these cases, unless the post involves substantial access to children.

Bibliography

Ackroyd, S., Harper, R., Hughes, J., Shapiro, D., Soothill, K. (1992), *New Technology and Practical Police Work* , Open University Press.

ACPO (Association of Chief Police Officers), (1987), *Code of Practice for Police Computer Systems*.

Adelman, S.E. (1990), 'Reevaluating Massachusetts criminal history record statute', in US Department of Justice *Juvenile and Adult Records: One System, One Record?*.

ADSS (Association of Directors of Social Services), (1992), Evidence to the Inquiry into the Selection and Recruitment of Staff in Childrens Homes.

Allen, F. (1981), *The Decline of the Rehabilitative Ideal,* Yale University Press.

AMA (Association of Metropolitan Authorities), (1990), '*Protection of children: disclosure of criminal background*', (Education Circular 15/90).

Apex Trust, (1989), *Making Rehabilitation Work.*

Apex Trust, (1990), *Realising the Potential: The Recruitment of People with a Criminal Record.*

Apex Trust, (1991), *The Hidden Workforce.*

Audit Commission, (1988), *Improving the Performance of the Fingerprint Service,* (Police Papers).

Babington, A. (1969), *A House in Bow Street: Crime and the Magistracy in London* ,1740-1881, MacDonald & Co.

Baldwin, J. & Houghton, J. (1986), 'Circular arguments: the status and legitimacy of administrative rules', *Public Law* pp239-284.

Baldwin-Edwards, M. (1991), 'Immigration after 1991', *Policy and Politics* 19(3).

Barton, S. (1990), 'Juvenile records and record keeping systems: summary of a national survey', in US Department of Justice, *Juvenile and Adult Records: One System, One Record?.*

Baxter, J.D. (1990), *State Security, Privacy and Information,* Harvester Wheatsheaf.

Belair, R. (1988), 'Public availability of criminal history records: a legal analysis', in *Open versus Confidential Records,* US Department of Justice, Washington DC.

Blumstein, A. (1984), 'Violent and career offender programs', in US Bureau of Justice Statistics, *Information Policy and Crime Control Strategies.*

Boseley, S. (1984), 'List of errors that ended in child's death', *The Guardian,* 18 December.

Botsford, K. (1990), 'Whiff of Salem in a loony state', *The Independent,* 3 March.

Bowden, P. (1985), 'Psychiatry and dangerousness: a counter renaissance?', in Gostin L. ed., *Secure Provision* ,Tavistock.

Bratt, A. (1970), 'Survey of state criminal justice information systems', in Project SEARCH ed., *Proceedings of a National Symposium on Criminal Justice and Statistics Systems.*

Breed, B. (nd), *Off the Record,* John Clare Books.

Brindle, D. (1989), 'Jobs with young shut to offenders', *The Guardian,* 30 August.

Brongersma, E. (1988), 'A defence of sexual liberty for all age groups', *The Howard Journal of Criminal Justice* ,27(1).

Bunyan, T. (1976), *The History and Practice of the Political Police in Britain,* J. Friedman.

Burnham, D. (1983), *The Rise of the Computer State,* Random House.

Calderdale MBC, (1989), *An Inquiry into the Appointment of Dr. R.A. Ryall to the Post of Director of Social Services.*

Campbell, D. (1980), 'Society under surveillance', in Hain P. ed *Policing the Police,* vol 1, John Calder.

Campbell, D. & Connor, S. (1986), *On the Record,* Joseph.

Carvel, J. (1989), 'Hurd signals move towards central intelligence unit', *The Guardian,* 27 September.

Cockburn, A. (1990), 'Abused imaginings', *New Statesman and Society,* 26 January.

Cohen, N. (1991), 'Civil rights fears over police DNA database', *The Independent,* 14 August.

Cohen, S. (1985), *Visions of Social Control,* Polity.

Commission of the European Communities (1990), *Proposal for a council directive concerning the protection of individuals in relation to the processing of personal data COM(90) 314 FINAL -SYN 287),* Brussels, 13 September.

Cosgrove, M. (1989), 'Take no risks with client care', *Community Care,* 28 September.

Council of Europe, (1981), *Convention for the Protection of Individuals with regard to Automatic Processing of Personal Data.*

Council of Europe, (1984), *The Criminal Record and Rehabilitation of Convicted Persons* Council of Europe.

Council of Europe, (1988), *Regulating the Use of Personal Data in the Police Sector Recommendation R(14)87, Council of Europe.*

Crane, P. (1984), *Gays and the Law,Pluto Press.*

Crow, I. (1987), 'Black people and criminal justice in the UK', *Howard Journal of Criminal Justice,* 26(4) pp 303-314.

Dandeker, C. (1990), *Surveillance, Power and Modernity,* Polity.

DENI (Dept. of Education Northern Ireland), (1990), 'Disclosure of criminal background of persons with access to children', (ref. Circular No.28/1990).

Dept. of Health, (1991b), *Registration of Childminding and Day Care,* HMSO.

Dept. of Health, (1991c), 'Disclosure of criminal background: proprietors and managers of residential care homes and nursing homes', (ref. LAC (91) 4).

Dept. of Health, (1991d), *Children Act 1989 Guidance and Regulations Vol. 4 Residential Care,* HMSO.

Dept. of Health, (1991e), *Children Act 1989 Guidance and Regulations Vol 3 Family Placements,* HMSO.

Dept. of Health, (1991f), *Children Act 1989 Guidance and Regulations Vol 5 Independent Schools*, HMSO.

Dept. of Health, (1991g), *Children Act 1989 The Welfare of Children in Boarding Schools – Practice Guidance,* HMSO.

Dept. of Health, (1991h), *Children in Public Care,* (SSI) HMSO.

DES (Dept. of Education and Science), (1987), 'Protection of children: disclosure of criminal background of those with access to children', (ref. No. RS 17/999).

DHSS (Dept. of Health and Social Security), (1974), *Report of the Committee of Inquiry into the Care and Supervision Provided in Relation to Maria Colwell ,* HMSO.

DHSS (Dept. of Health and Social Security), (1976), 'Non-accidental injury to children: the police and case conferences', (ref. LASSL (76) 26).

DHSS (Dept. of Health and Social Security), (1977), *A Guide to Adoption Practice (Advisory Council on Child Care No.2,* HMSO.

DHSS (Dept. of Health and Social Security), (1978), 'Release of prisoners convicted of offences against young children in the home', (ref. LAC (78) 22).

DHSS (Dept. of Health and Social Security), (1984), *Report of the Committee of Inquiry into Human Fertilisation and Embryology,* (The Warnock Report), HMSO.

DHSS (Dept. of Health and Social Security), (1984), 'Adoption agency regulations', (ref. LAC (84) 3).

DHSS (Dept. of Health and Social Security), (1987), *Reports to Court: Practice Guidance for Social Workers*, HMSO.

DHSS (Dept of Health and Social Security), (1988), 'Protection of children: disclosure of criminal background of those with access to children', (ref. HC (88) 9).

DHSS NI (Dept. of Health and Social Security: Northern Ireland), (1989), 'Disclosure of criminal background of persons seeking access to children or mentally handicapped people', (ref. A556/89).

Douglas, G., Hebenton, B. & Thomas, T. (1992) 'The right to found a family', *New Law Journal* vol 142 No. 6547, No.6548.

Downing, D. (1985), *'Employer Biases Toward Hiring and Placement of Male Ex-Offenders'*, Ph.D. dissertation, University of Southern Illinois, USA.

Downs, D. (1967), *Inside Bureaucracy,* Little, Brown & Co.

DPR (Data Protection Registrar), (1989), *The use of subject access provisions of the Data Protection Act to check the criminal records of applicants for jobs or licenses*, Guidance Note No.21.

DPR (Data Protection Registrar), (1991), *Seventh Annual Report*, HMSO.

DPR (Data Protection Registrar), (1992), *Eighth Annual Report* ,HMSO.

Draper, H. (1978), *Private Police*, Harvester.

Dworkin, R. (1990), *A Bill of Rights for Britain, Chatto & Windus.*

Ellul, J. (1964), *The Technological Society,* Vintage Books.

Enright, S. & Morton, J. (1990), *Taking Liberties: The Criminal Jury in the 1990s*, Weidenfeld & Nicholson.

European Commission, (1991), *Treaty on Political Union*.

Evans, R. and Wilkinson, C. (1990), 'Variations in police cautioning policy and practice in England and Wales', *Howard Journal of Criminal Justice,* 29(3).

Farrington, D. (1981), 'Longitudinal research on crime and delinquency *British Journal of Criminology*, 21(1) pp 173-175.

Farrington, D. (1989), 'The origins of crime: the Cambridge study of delinquent development', *Home Office Research and Planning Unit Bulletin,* No.27.

Finkelhor, D., Williams, L.M., and Burns, N. (1988), *Nursery Crimes* Sage.

Flaherty,D. (1986a), 'Governmental surveillance and bureaucratic accountability: data protection agencies in western societies', *Science, Technology and Human Values* ,11(1).

Flaherty, D. (1986b), 'Protecting privacy in police information systems: data protection in the Canadian police information centre', *University of Toronto Law Journal*.

Foreign and Commonwealth Affairs Office, (1991), *European Convention on Mutual Assistance in Criminal Matters Cm 1928* ,HMSO.

Foucault, M. (1979), *Discipline and Punish: The Birth of the Prison* ,Penguin.

Fraser, G.P.A. (1981), 'The applications of police computing', in Pope, D.W. & Weiner, N.L. eds *Modern Policing,* Croom Helm.

Fry, A. (1989), 'Top people must be vetted', *Social Work Today,* 14 September.

Ganz,G. (1987), *Quasi-Legislation: Recent Developments in Secondary Legislation,* Sweet & Maxwell.

Genz, M. (1980), 'Employers', use of criminal records under Title VII', *Catholic University Law Review,* 29 pp597-623.

Giddens, A. (1981), *A Contemporary Critique of Historical Materialism Vol 1,* Macmillan.

Giddens, A. (1987), 'Nation-states and violence', in *Social Theory and Modern Sociology,* Polity.

Gordon, D. (1986), 'The electronic panopticon: a case study of the development of the national criminal records system', *Politics and Society,* 15(3) pp483-511.

Gordon, D. (1990), *The Justice Juggernaut,* Rutgers University Press.

Gordon, P. (1988), 'Black people and the criminal law', *International Journal of the Sociology of Law,* 16(3) pp295-315.

Gostin, L. (1984), *A Practical Guide to Mental Health Law,* MIND.

Gutman,J. (1982), 'The abuses of police records', *Center Magazine,* September/October pp56-63.

Harvey, L. & Pease, K. (1988), 'Custodial careers in the UK', in Harrison A. & Gretton J. eds *Crime UK 1988,* Polity Journals.

Heal, K., Tarling, R., & Burrows, J. (1985), *Policing Today,* HMSO.

Hebenton, B. & Thomas, T. (1989), 'Information or gossip?', *Community Care,* 26 January.

Hebenton, B. & Thomas, T. (1990), 'Approved households: checking criminal records', *Adoption and Fostering,* 14 (2).

Hebenton,B. & Thomas,T. (1992), 'The police and social services departments in England and Wales: the exchange of personal information', *Journal of Social Welfare and Family Law*, No.2.

Herrington,L.H. (1986), 'The unspeakable must be spoken', in US Department of Justice, *Data Quality Policies and Practice.*

HFEA (Human Fertilisation and Embryology Authority), (1991(a)), *Code of Practice: Consultative Document.*

HFEA (Human Fertilisation and Embryology Authority), (1991(b)),.*Code of Practice: Explanation.*

HFEA (Human Fertilisation and Embryology Authority), (1991(c)),. *Code of Practice.*

Home Office, (1954), 'Convictions on teachers', (ref. HOC 151/1954).

Home Office/Lord Chancellors Dept., (1961), *Report of the Interdepartmental Committee on the Business of the Criminal Courts Cmnd 1289*, (The Streatfield Report).

Home Office, (1964), 'Children and Young Person Act 1963: Parts I and III', (ref. Circular No.22/1964).

Home Office, (1975), 'Rehabilitation of Offenders Act 1974', (ref. Circular No.98/1975).

Home Office, (1978), 'Citing of Police Cautions in the Juvenile Court', (ref. Circular No.49/1978).

Home Office, (1982), 'Disclosure of convictions to local authorities in respect of prospective childminders', (ref. Circular No.105/1982).

Home Office, (1985a), 'Criminal careers of those born in 1953, 1958, and 1963', *Home Office Statistical Bulletin No.7.*

Home Office/DIISS, (1985b), Disclosure of Criminal Convictions of Those with Access to Children, First Report.

Home Office, (1986a), 'Police Reports of Convictions and Related Information', (ref. Circular No.45/1986).

Home Office, (1986b), 'Protection of children: disclosure of criminal background of those with access to children', (ref. Circular No.44/1986).

Home Office, (1986c), Consolidated Circular to the Police on Crime and Kindred Matters.

Home Office, (1986d), 'Social inquiry reports', (ref. Circular No.92/1986).

Home Office, (1988a), *Enforcement of Jury Disqualifications*, (ref. Circular No.43/1988).

Home Office, (1988b), 'Protection of children: disclosure of criminal background of those with access to children', (ref. Circular No.102/1988).

Home Office, (1989a), 'Press access to court lists and the register of decisions in magistrates'courts', (ref. Circular No.90/1989).

Home Office, (1989b), 'Protection of children: disclosure of criminal background of those with access to children', (ref. Circular No.58/1989).

Home Office, (1990a), *Government Reply to 3rd Report from Home Affairs Committee Session 1989-90*, Cm 1163 HMSO.

Home Office, (1990b), 'The cautioning of offenders', (ref. Circular No.59/1990).

Home Office, (1990c), *Future Computer Systems for Magistrates Courts the MASS Project*, (C2 Division).

Home Office, (1990d), *The Sentence of the Court* ,(5th ed.) HMSO.

Home Office, (1990e), 'Provision for mentally disordered offenders', (ref. Circular No.66/1990).

Home Office, (1990f), *Report of the Committee on Privacy and Related Matters Cm 1102,* HMSO.

Home Office, (1990g), *Criminal Statistics England and Wales Cmnd 1322,* HMSO.

Home Office, (1991), *The National Collection of Criminal Records: Report of an Efficiency Scrutiny.*

Home Office, (1992), *The National Criminal Intelligence Service*, (Note by the Home Office to the AMA), January.

House of Commons, (1990a), *Criminal Records* Home Affairs Committee 3rd report Session 1989-90, HMSO.

House of Commons, (1990b), *Practical Police Co-operation in the European Community,* Home Affairs Committee, 7th report, Session 1989-90, HMSO.

House of Commons, (1991), *Recruitment Practices Employment Committee 2nd Report Session 1990-91, HMSO.*

Howard League, (1985), *Unlawful Sex,* Waterlow.

Hudson, B. (1989), *'Discrimination and disparity: researching the influence of race on sentencing'*, Paper presented to the British Criminology Conference, Bristol.

Hyder, K. (1988), 'The child care vetting crisis', *Police Review* 5 August.

Johnston, L. (1992), 'Regulating Private Security', International Journal of Sociology of Law, 20 pp1-16.

Kahan, B. & Levy, A. (1991), *The Pindown Experience and the Protection of Children,* Staffordshire County Council.

Kendall, R. (1989), 'Computerization in the General Secretariat', *International Criminal Police Review*, November/December.

Kenilworth Group, (1989), *Making the Most of Volunteers*.

Kenney, J. (1964), *The California State Police,* Charles C. Thomas.

King, M.(1981), *The Framework of Criminal Justice,* Croom Helm.

Kirby, T. (1990), 'Chief constables disagree on FBI-style crime unit', *The Independent,* 19 January.

Laudon, K. (1986), *The Dossier Society: Value Choices in the Design of National Information Systems,* Columbia University Press.

LEAA (Law Enforcement Assistance Administration), (1981) *Privacy and Security of Criminal History Information.*

Leigh, D. (1980), *The Frontiers of Secrecy,* Junction Books.

Leuba, P. (1988), 'Demand for criminal history records by noncriminal justice agencies', in US Department of Justice, *Open vs. Confidential Records.*

Lincoln, A. (1989), 'Background checks', *Library & Archival Security,* 9(3/4) pp107-113.

Lloyd-Bostock, S. (1988), *Law in Practice,* Routledge.

London Borough of Islington, (1989), *Liam Johnstone Review: Report of a Panel of Inquiry.*

London Borough of Lambeth, (1987), *Whose Child?.*

Lord Chancellor's Department, (1992), *Court Service Annual Report*, HMSO.

Lustgarten, L. *(1986), Governance of Police,* Sweet & Maxwell.

Lynch, J. (1986), 'Taking the lid off Kincora', *Community Care,* 4 December.

MacDonald, E. (1990), 'A shocking abuse of trust', *The Independent on Sunday,* 15 July.

Manchester, C. (1990), 'Liquor licensing and applicants with criminal records', *Justice of the Peace,* 27 October.

Marchand, D. (1980), *The Politics of Privacy, Computers, and Criminal Justice Records,* Information Resources Press.

Marks, K. & Whitfield, M. (1992), 'Police checks on nannies urged to prevent abuse', *The Independent,* 26 March.

Marx, G.(1985), 'I'll be watching you', *Dissent,* Winter: 26-34.

Mason, G. (1992), 'NCIS is ready to go', *Police Review,* 27 March.

McLeod, N. (1991) 'English DNA evidence held inadmissible', *Criminal Law Review,* 583-590.

McWilliams, W.& Pease, K. (1990), 'Probation practice and an end to punishment', *Howard Journal of Criminal Justice,* 29(1): 14-25.

Melossi, D. (1976), 'Institutions of social control and the capitalist organization of work: some hypotheses for research, *La Questione Criminale,* 2/3 (11).

Miller, A.(1972), *The Assault on Privacy* ,New American Library.

Mills,H. (1989), 'Council did not check background of rapist', *The Independent,* 11 July.

Ministry of Health, (1968), 'Health services and public health act 1968', (ref. Circular 36/1968).

Mitchell, D.(1989), 'Mellor pilots vetting for voluntary workers', *Community Care,* 3 August.

Molle,W. (1990), *The Economics of European Integration,* Dartmouth Publishing Co.

NACRO (National Association for the Care and Resettlement of Offenders), (1986), *Black People and the Criminal Justice System.*

NACRO (National Association for the Care and Resettlement of Offenders), (1990), *Declaring Convictions.*

NCCL (National Council for Civil Liberties) (1988), *Identity Cards and the Threat to Civil Liberties,* Briefing Paper.

NCCL (National Council for Civil Liberties), (1988), 'NCCL urges reform of police checks system', (Press release).

NCCL (National Council for Civil Liberties), (1990), *Submission to the Employment Committee on Employers Recruitment Practices (Pre-employment vetting).*

NCCL (National Council for Civil Liberties), (1991), *Report on the Criminal Record and Information System.*

Nelson,D. (1992), 'Five face charges over claims of child abuse', *The Independent,* 16 March.

Newing, J. (1987), 'Up-dating the PNC', *Policing* ,Winter.

Newing, J. (1990), 'Information technology for the improvement of policing', *International Criminal Police Review,* September-October: 13-15.

Norton-Taylor, R. (1989), 'Kincora scandal lingers on', *The Guardian,* 23 October.

Nugter, A.C.M. (1990), *Transborder Flow of Personal Data within the EC,* Kluwer.

Office of Technology Assessment, (1982), *An Assessment of Alternatives for a National Computerized Criminal History System* Washington DC.

Ogden, J. (1992), 'Inquiry finds growing problems in Homes', *Social Work Today* 30 April.

O'Sullivan,J. & Jones,J. (1991), 'Head of children's homes jailed for life, five times', *The Independent* 30 November.

Oulton,C. & Naylor, S. (1992), 'Nanny jailed for fracturing two babies's skulls', *The Independent* 9 January.

Pape, R. (1992), *CCCJS – state of the art review* Home Office 24 March.

Parton, N. (1985), *The Politics of Child Abuse* Macmillan.

Platt, S. (1988), 'Police check delays put children at risk', *New Society,* 19 February.

Poggi, G. (1978), *The Development of the Modern State,* Hutchinson.

Poggi, G. (1990), *The State: Its Nature, Development and Prospects,* Polity.

PCMG (Police Checks Monitoring Group), (1988), *There is a Better Way.*

PCA (Police Complaints Authority), (1991), *Annual Report of the Police Complaints Authority,* HMSO.

Prince, L. (1982), 'Police and employee vetting', *Police Review,* 90 No.2320.

Pringle, P. (1955), *Hue and Cry,* Museum Press.

Radzinowicz, L. & Hood, R. (1990), *The Emergence of Penal Policy in Victorian and Edwardian England*, Clarendon Press.

Rankin, M. (1989), 'Screening offends me', *Involve*, No 63.

Reed,C. (1990), 'Child abuse allegations that are threatening to ruin a community', *The Guardian,* 2 August.

Rickford, F. (1991), 'Welcome home', *Social Work Today*, 21 November.

Rose, N. (1990), *Governing the Soul,* Routledge.

Rotman, E. (1986), 'Do criminal offenders have a constitutional right to rehabilitation?', *Journal of Criminal Law and Criminology*, 77 (Winter) pp1023-1028.

Rule, J. (1973), *Private Lives and Public Surveillance,* Allen Lane.

Rule, J., McAdam, D., Stearns, L., Uglow, D. (1980), 'Preserving individual autonomy in an information-oriented society', in Hoffman L.J. ed. *Computers and Privacy in the Next Decade,* Academic Press.

Schengen Convention, (1990) *Applying the Schengen Agreement of 14 June 1985 between the Governments of the Benelux Economic Union, the Federal Republic of Germany and the French Republic on the gradual abolition of checks at their common borders ,*June.

Scottish Education Dept., (1989), 'Protection of children: disclosure of criminal convictions of those with access to children: local authorities', (ref.Circular No. SW9/1989).

SEARCH Group, (1970), *Proceedings of the National Symposium on Criminal Justice Information and Statistics Systems,* California Technological Research Foundation.

SEARCH Group, (1975), *Technical Report No.13, Standards for Security and Privacy of Criminal Justice Information.*

SEARCH Group, (1979), *Federal Access to State and Local Criminal Justice Information.*

SEARCH Group, (1984), *Compendium of State Privacy and Security Legislation.*

SEARCH Group, (1987), *Compendium of State Privacy and Security Legislation.*

SEARCH Group, (1988), *Technical Report No.13 (Revised), Standards for the Security and Privacy of Criminal History Record Information.*

Shaw, L. & Lobo, D. (1989), 'Criminal career of those born in 1953, 1958 and 1963 *Home Office Research and Planning Unit Bulletin,* No.27.

Smith, D.J. & Gray, J. (1983), *Police and People in London,* IV Policy Studies Institute.

Solzhenitsyn, A. (1971), *Cancer Ward,* Penguin.

Sone, K. (1991), 'Slipping through the net', *Community Care,* 5th December, pp14-16.

South, N. (1988), *Policing for Profit,* Sage.

Spencer, M. (1990), *1992 and All That,* Civil Liberties Trust.

SSI (Social Services Inspectorate), (1989), 'Protection of children: disclosure of criminal background of those with access to children – agency staff', (ref. C1(89)16).

Statewatch, (1992), 'Privacy protection needed', 2(1) January/February.

Summers, W.C. (1986), 'Law enforcement efforts to improve data quality of criminal history records', in US Department of Justice *Data Quality Policies and Procedures,* Washington DC.

SWSG (Social Work Services Group), (1985), 'Disclosure of criminal convictions of those with access to children', (Consultation Paper)', November 1985.

Tarling, R. & Burrows, J. (1985), 'The work of detectives', in Heal K. et al *Policing Today,* HMSO.

Taylor, I. (1981), *Law and Order: Arguments for Socialism*, Macmillan.

Taylor, J. & Williams, H. (1991), 'Public administration and the information polity', *Public Administration*, 69 (2).

Thomas, T. (1989), 'Social work students and criminal record checks', *Social Work Education* 8(3).

Thomas, T. & Hebenton, B. (1990), 'One of us: Britain's growing army', *Criminal Justice,* 8(1): 10-12.

Thomas, T. & Hebenton, B. (1991a), 'Disclosure of criminal records: a comparative review', *Police Studies,* 14(2): 51-62.

Thomas, T. & Hebenton, B. (1991b), 'To minimize future risk: Circular 88(102) and the politics of protection', *Journal of Social Welfare and Family Law,* No.2.

Thorpe, D.H., Smith, D., Green, C.J., & Paley, J.H. (1980), *Out of Care,* George Allen & Unwin.

Unell, J. (1992), *Criminal Records Checks within the Voluntary Sector: An Evaluation of the Pilot Schemes,* Volunteer Centre UK.

US Congress Senate, (1974), *Criminal Justice Databanks 1974:* vol 1 93d Cong, 2d session.

US Department of Justice, (1981), *Privacy and the Private Employer.*

US Department of Justice, (1987), *Correctional Populations in the United States 1985,* Bureau of Justice Statistics.

US Department of Justice, (1988), *Public Access to Criminal History Record Information.*

Visher, A. & Roth, J. (1986), 'Criminal careers', in Blumstein A. ed. *Criminal Careers and Career Criminals,* National Academy Press.

Von Hirsch, A. (1981), 'Desert and previous convictions in sentencing', *Minnesota Law Review*, 65: 591-593.

Von Hirsch, A. (1986), *Past or Future Crimes,* Manchester University Press.

Wadsworth, M. (1979), *The Roots of Delinquency,* Martin Robertson.

Walker, N. (1985), *Sentencing: Theory, Law and Practice,* Butterworth.

Wasik, M. (1987), 'Guidance, guidelines and criminal record', in Wasik, M. & Pease, K. eds *Sentencing Reform: Guidance or Guidelines,* Manchester University Press.

Wasik, M. & Pease, K. eds (1987), *Sentencing Reform: Guidance or Guidelines,* Manchester University Press.

Wasserman, G. (1989), 'Putting crime into context – interview', *Siemens Magazine* : com 5/89.

Waters, R. (1991), *Ethnic Minorities and the Criminal Justice System.* Avebury.

Waugh, P. (1991), 'The use of computers in the administration of justice in the UK', in *Yearbook of Law, Computers and Technology vol 5.*

Westin, A. & Baker, M. (1972), *Databanks in a Free Society*. Quadrangle Books.

Wheeler, S. (1969), 'Problems and issues in record-keeping', in: Wheeler, S. ed *On Record: Files and Dossiers in American Life,* Russell Sage Foundation.

Whitcher, A. & Jones, V. (1989), *Police Checks: A Survey,* Volunteer Centre UK/NAVB.

Wilson, T. (1988), 'Public availability of criminal history records: a policy analysis', in US Department of justice, *Open vs Confidential Records*.

Working Mothers Association, (1992), *Day Care in the Home*.

Yearley, S. (1988), *Science, Technology and Social Change,* Unwin Hyman.

Zenk, G. (1979) *Project SEARCH,* Greenwood Press.

Index

Bow Street, 13

Italy, 76

National Football Intelligence Unit, 48

National Identification Bureau (NIB), 6, 40-41, 43-47, 55-57, 68, 95, 144, 149
   national criminal record office, 43
   national fingerprint office, 43

National Office for the Suppression of Counterfeit Currency, 48

National Paedophile Index, 48

Norway, 76, 82

Nurseries and Childminders Regulations Act 1948, 120

penal servitude, 14, 21

Penal Servitude Act 1864, 14

police, 3
   criminal intelligence, 3, 4
   regional services advisory committee, 25

Police Act 1964, 26

Police Complaints Authority, 60

Police and Criminal Evidence Act 1984, 41, 67, 72, 85

Police Gazette, 18, 22, 23, 47

Police National Computer (PNC), 41, 42-43, 44, 47, 55, 58, 68, 86, 144, 146

politics of protection, 10

Poor Law Amendment Act 1834, 14

pornography, 4

Powers of Criminal Courts Act 1973, 77

press, 81-82
   Complaints Commission, 82

Prevention of Crimes Act, 1871 16, 18, 20-21, 40, 85

prisons, 14, 73-74, 83

private detectives, 6